A Christmas Carol

by Charles Dickens

Authors and Series Editors:
Sue Bennett and Dave Stockwin

HODDER
EDUCATION
AN HACHETTE UK COMPANY

608

The publisher would like to thank the following for permission to reproduce copyright material:

Photo credits:

p. 8 Georgios Kollidas/Fotolia; **p. 10** nickolae/Fotolia; **p. 12** © Pictorial Press Ltd/Alamy; **pp. 19, 28, 31, 38** TopFoto; **p. 40** Arthur Rackham/Mary Evans Picture Library; **p. 71** Ingram

Although every effort has been made to ensure that website addresses are correct at time of going to press, Hodder Education cannot be held responsible for the content of any website mentioned. It is sometimes possible to find a relocated web page by typing in the address of the home page for a website in the URL window of your browser.

Orders: please contact Bookpoint Ltd, 130 Park Drive, Milton Park, Abingdon, Oxon OX14 4SE. Telephone: (44) 01235 827720. Fax: (44) 01235 400454. Lines are open 9.00–17.00, Monday to Saturday, with a 24-hour message answering service. Visit our website at www.hoddereducation.co.uk

© Sue Bennett and Dave Stockwin 2016

First published in 2016 by

Hodder Education

An Hachette UK Company,

Carmelite House, 50 Victoria Embankment

London EC4Y 0LS

Impression number	5	4	3	2	1
Year		2020	2019	2018	2017	2016

Cover photo: © Getty Images/Cultura RM

Typeset in Bliss Light 11/13 by Integra Software Services Pvt. Ltd., Pondicherry, India.

Printed in Italy

A catalogue record for this title is available from the British Library

ISBN 9781471853524

Contents

Getting the most from this guide

This guide is designed to help you to raise your achievement in your examination response to *A Christmas Carol*. It is intended for you to use throughout your GCSE English literature course. It will help you when you are studying the novel for the first time and also during your revision.

The following features have been used throughout this guide to help you focus your understanding of the novel:

Target your thinking

A list of **introductory questions** is provided at the beginning of each chapter to give you a breakdown of the material covered, labelled by Assessment Objective. They target your thinking in order to help you work more efficiently by focusing on the key messages.

Build critical skills

These offer an opportunity to consider some **more challenging questions**. They are designed to encourage deeper thinking, analysis and exploratory thought. Building and practising critical skills in this way will give you a real advantage in the examination.

GRADE *FOCUS*

It is possible to know a novel well and yet still underachieve in the examination if you are unsure of what the examiners are looking for. The **GRADE FOCUS** boxes give a clear explanation of how you may be assessed, with an emphasis on the criteria for gaining a grade 5 and a grade 8.

REVIEW YOUR LEARNING

At the end of each chapter you will find the Review your learning section to **test your knowledge:** a series of short specific questions to ensure that you have understood and absorbed the key messages of the chapter. Answers to the Review your learning questions are provided in the final section of the guide.

GRADE *BOOSTER*

Read and remember this **grade-boosting advice:** top tips from experienced teachers and examiners who can advise you on what to do, as well as what not to do, to maximise your chances of success in the examination.

Key quotation

Key quotations are highlighted for you, so that if you wish you may use them as **supporting evidence** in your examination answers. Further quotations grouped by characterisation, key moments and theme can be found in the Top ten quotations section towards the end of the guide. Page references are given for the 1993 Parragon edition of the text.

'I don't make merry myself at Christmas and I can't afford to make idle people merry.' (p. 13)

Introduction

Studying the text

You may find it useful to read sections of this guide when you need them, rather than reading it from start to finish. For example, the Context section can be read before you read the novel itself, since it offers an explanation of relevant historical, cultural and literary background to the text. It is here where you will find information about aspects of Dickens's life and times which influenced his writing, the particular issues with which Dickens was concerned and where the novel stands in terms of the literary tradition to which it belongs.

As you work through the novel, you may find it helpful to read the relevant pages of the Plot and structure section before or after reading a particular chapter. As well as a summary of events there is also commentary, so that you are aware both of key events and features in each of the staves. The sections on characterisation, on themes and on language, style and analysis will help to develop your thinking further, in preparation for written responses on particular aspects of the text.

Many students also enjoy the experience of being able to bring something extra to their classroom lessons in order to be 'a step ahead of the game'. Alternatively, you may have missed a classroom session or feel that you need a clearer explanation and the guide can help you with this too.

An initial reading of the section on Assessment Objectives and skills will enable you to make really effective notes in preparation for assessments. The Assessment Objectives are what examination boards base their mark schemes on. In this section they are broken down and clearly explained.

Revising the text

Whether you study the novel in a block of time close to the exam or much earlier in your GCSE literature course, you will need to revise thoroughly if you are to achieve the very best grade that you can.

You should first remind yourself of what happens in the novel and so the Plot and structure section might be returned to in the first instance. You might then look at the Assessment Objectives and skills section to ensure that you understand what the examiners are looking for in general, and then look carefully at the Tackling the exams section.

This section gives you useful information on question format, depending on which examination board specification you are following, as well as practical advice on the examination format, and practical considerations such as the time available for the question and the Assessment

Objectives which apply to it. Advice is also supplied on how to approach the question, writing a quick plan, and 'working' the text, since all of the examination boards use an extract based question for *A Christmas Carol*.

Focused advice on how you might improve your grade follows, and you need to read this section carefully.

You will also find examples of exam-style responses in the Sample essays section, with examiner's comments in the margins, so that you can see clearly how to move towards a grade 5 and how to then move from grade 5 to grade 8.

Now that all GCSE literature examinations are 'closed book', the Top ten section will be an invaluable aid in that it offers you the opportunity to learn short quotations to support points about character and themes as well as being a revision aid which identifies ten quotations in the transformation of Scrooge.

When writing about the novel, use this guide as a springboard to develop your own ideas. Remember: the examiners are not looking for set responses. You should not read this guide in order to memorise chunks of it, ready to regurgitate in the exam. Identical answers are dull. The examiners hope to reward you for perceptive thought, individual appreciation and varying interpretations. They want to sense you have engaged with the themes and ideas in the novel, explored Dickens's methods with an awareness of the context in which he wrote and enjoyed this part of your literature course.

There are, of course, a number of film versions of *A Christmas Carol*, ranging from the classic black and white film starring Alastair Sim to the recent Jim Carrey extravaganza, not to mention *The Muppet Christmas Carol* (which is surprisingly close to the text in places). However, you will find differences to the text in all of them, For example, in the Muppets version there are two Marleys, one of whom is called Robert! All of these are enjoyable versions of the tale which convey the essential message of the novel. However, they should never be seen as a substitute for the text itself. Examiners are unlikely to be impressed by responses which refer to songs in *A Christmas Carol*, or claim that Marley's first name is Bob!

Enjoy referring to the guide as you study the text, and good luck in your exam.

Target your thinking

- What is meant by 'context'? (**AO3**)
- How did Dickens's life influence his work? (**AO3**)
- How did socioeconomic conditions in the nineteenth century inform Dickens's work? (**AO3**)
- What was London like in the time of Dickens? (**AO3**)
- How was Christmas celebrated? (**AO3**)
- Did Dickens believe in ghosts? (**AO3**)

What is context?

Knowledge of context will help you to understand and appreciate your reading of *A Christmas Carol*, but what exactly is it?

Context is a wide-ranging term. It refers to the historical, socioeconomic and political circumstances of the time, as well as the author's beliefs about those circumstances. It also refers to the way that more personal events in the author's own life may have influenced the author's thinking and writing, in this case Charles Dickens. Finally, it may also refer to literary context and be concerned with developments in the novel as a form which may also have influenced the way it was written.

Dickens's life

▲ Charles Dickens

Charles John Huffam Dickens was born on 7 February 1812 in Portsmouth, the second of eight children. He spent much of his childhood in London, living for some time in Camden, in a house which has been said to have been the inspiration for the Cratchit family home. His family was not well off and, like Peter Cratchit, 'he might have known, and very likely did, the inside of a pawnbroker's' (p. 57). In 1824 his father was imprisoned for non-payment of a baker's bill, so the young Dickens had direct experience of the horror of debt, illustrated in *A Christmas Carol* by the fear and anxiety of the gentle Caroline and her family.

At the age of 12, he was sent to work in a blacking factory, and this experience left him with an understanding and sympathy for the poor, and for poor children in particular, which stayed with him for the rest of his life.

He married in 1836 and for a while the marriage was happy. The depictions of marriage and family life in *A Christmas Carol*, written in 1843, are overwhelmingly positive. Belle and her husband, the Fezziwigs, the Cratchits and Caroline and her husband all illustrate a cosy picture of domestic bliss.

However, in later years Dickens fell out of love with his wife, who he felt had aged prematurely and was exhausted by child bearing — Dickens and his wife had ten children. Dickens began to pursue younger and prettier women, notably the actress, Nelly Ternan, with whom it is believed that he had a passionate, though secret, affair.

He was hugely successful and respected in his lifetime as a writer, an entertainer and a social commentator. He loved touring and reading his novels to appreciative audiences and the prospect of this undoubtedly influenced his narrative style. Today, his novels are still widely read, loved and frequently adapted for film, stage and television.

A Christmas Carol is the most frequently adapted of them all, with the name 'Scrooge' having passed into the English language as a general term for a miser.

Dickens wrote 18 novels and was working on a nineteenth when he died in 1870.

Dickens's London

The setting for *A Christmas Carol* is Victorian London, which was in many ways a very different place to the city we know today. There was perhaps a greater, more conspicuous sense of community for some, as can be seen from the vibrant descriptions of the Christmas shops, the people turning out in their best clothes to go to church and chapel, to visit relatives or to slide and throw snowballs or to carry their dinners to the bakers' shops. Poor people had open fires to heat their homes and cook on, but no ovens. Bakers opened their shops on Sundays and holidays and charged a small fee to cook people's dinners. In *A Christmas Carol,* the Cratchit children fetch the goose from the baker's for their Christmas lunch.

Key quotation

But, if you had judged from the numbers of people on their way to friendly gatherings, you might have thought that no one was at home to give them welcome when they got there, instead of every house expecting company, and piling its fires half-chimney high. (p. 58)

However, there was also a darker side to the city. The nineteenth century was a time of great social change, and with that change came many social problems. The Industrial Revolution transformed England from a mainly rural economy to an industrial one, with thousands of poor country people flocking to the cities in search of work.

Without an infrastructure to support them, many were forced to live in insanitary and overcrowded conditions. The alleys and courts of the city were dark and dirty, and often associated with crime and degeneracy, particularly after sundown. Dickens uses Stave 4 of *A Christmas Carol* in particular to raise awareness of this, when Scrooge is taken to the area of old Joe's shop.

Key quotation

Alleys and archways, like so many cesspools, disgorged their offences of smell, and dirt, and life, upon the straggling streets; and the whole quarter reeked with crime, with filth, and misery. (p. 71)

▲ An alley in Victorian London, depicted by Gustave Doré

Today we are used to brightly illuminated homes, streets and workplaces but in Dickens's time people relied mainly on feeble gaslight, oil lamps and candles, so that the difference between night and day was much more marked, and night was seen as a time of lawlessness, mystery and fear. In *A Christmas Carol* light and dark are used very effectively to create atmosphere and reveal character.

Widespread pollution in the capital from unregulated factories merged with fog to create smog, which meant it was often very difficult to see. In Stave 1 'people ran about with flaring links' (p. 14) to offer their services in showing the way to carriages.

Dickens spent many hours walking around the streets of London in the middle of the night while writing the novel. This may have partly inspired his descriptions of Scrooge's nocturnal trips with the spirits.

Dickens and education

Although schools in nineteenth century literature were often seen as grim places where children suffered both cruelty and injustice, such as those in *Nicholas Nickleby* and *Hard Times*, Dickens believed passionately in the importance of education as the only way out of the cycle of deprivation in which many children were trapped.

For example, although Dickens presents Scrooge's experience of school as a lonely and unhappy one, Scrooge appears to have been greatly comforted by his ability to read about the adventures of Ali Baba. This early love of reading seems to have exerted a lasting influence on the elderly Scrooge, as its recollection creates in him a state of huge excitement. These tales were a great favourite of Dickens himself as a child.

Furthermore, in Stave 3 of *A Christmas Carol*, in what is one of the most powerful moments in the book, Ignorance and Want appear in the shape of two hideous children, of whom Scrooge is told to beware, especially of the boy named Ignorance, for on his forehead one word appears, 'Doom'.

Dickens's social conscience

In Dickens's time, the gap between rich and poor was much wider than it is today. Life for the poor was very difficult. Poor living conditions and lack of health care led to the spread of disease, high infant mortality and early death in adults. Workers had few rights, were poorly paid, and there was little job security. Scrooge's threat of dismissal to Bob in Stave 1 was a very real one.

If you could not support yourself, you could be taken into the workhouse, an institution supported by the Poor Law and feared by all. Once inside, it was very difficult to leave. You could be separated from your family, worked relentlessly and half-starved.

Attitudes to the poor were generally very harsh in Victorian England, because it was often assumed that if you were poor, it was your own fault. Scrooge's callous comments about the less fortunate were not untypical. When told by the charity collectors that many of the poor would rather die than go into the workhouse, Scrooge's response is: 'If they would rather die...they had better do it and decrease the surplus population' (p. 13).

There are critics who see the echoing of these words by the Ghost of Christmas Present as the key to understanding Dickens's economic philosophy. It has been argued that Scrooge may represent the ideas of Thomas Robert Malthus, a Victorian economist, one of whose beliefs was that population growth would always outpace food supply, resulting in inevitable poverty and starvation for the 'surplus population'. The implication is that the practical solution would be to allow that 'surplus population' to die.

Build critical skills

How is darkness associated with Scrooge in Stave 1 and in the 'death' of Scrooge in Stave 4, and to what effect?

Build critical skills

What do you think Dickens was suggesting by the use of the word 'Doom'?

▲ Victorian workhouse — these institutions were difficult to leave and feared by all

Dickens was very concerned by the callous treatment of the poor, and was prompted to take action after having read a report by the Children's Employment Commission, which shockingly revealed the poverty and cruelty faced by children employed in mines and factories. As well as this, he was deeply affected by a visit to the Field Lane Ragged School and a trip to an institution in Manchester devoted to caring for the poor.

He planned to publish a pamphlet called, 'An Appeal to the People of England, on behalf of the Poor Man's Child', but changed his mind and wrote *A Christmas Carol* instead, believing that a story pulling at the heartstrings of his readers would have 'twenty thousand times the force' that he could exert in a political pamphlet (as he put it in a letter of 1843).

Literary context

A Christmas Carol is not an easy novel to categorise. In some ways, it resembles the social realist novels of the time which reflected the harsh living conditions for many. It also has a central protagonist who moves from a state of ignorance and miserly selfishness to a state of paternal benevolence. This is typical of many nineteenth-century novels which involve a series of events or encounters that lead the central character towards the development of a new moral understanding. This is the case in *Great Expectations* also by Dickens, in George Eliot's *Silas Marner* and in Thomas Hardy's *The Mayor of Casterbridge*.

Other readers have commented that *A Christmas Carol* has elements of a fairy tale with the three spirits and the magic element of flight over the city, while for others the allegorical nature of the tale, wherein Scrooge symbolises all greedy and unfeeling businessmen and Bob represents the respectable poor, is the interpretation which is foremost in their minds.

However, it is also a ghost story, and can be seen as part of the Urban Gothic tradition which was so popular with the Victorians, and included novels such as R. L. Stevenson's *The Strange Case of Dr Jekyll and Mr Hyde*. In *A Christmas Carol* ghosts inhabit the city streets rather than castles in the depths of a forest in a foreign land. If you are interested in the genre, you may be able to think of modern examples of Urban Gothic stories since this genre's popularity has grown in recent times.

Dickens himself may have seen it more as a traditional winter tale to be read around the fireside with all the family on a cold evening. This meant that it needed to thrill readers without terrifying them, and there had to be a happy ending rather than a disturbing one.

In the preface to the original edition Dickens wrote:

> I have endeavoured in this Ghostly little book, to raise the Ghost of an Idea which shall not put my readers out of humour with themselves, with each other, with the season or with me. May it haunt their houses pleasantly, and no-one wish to lay it.

Dickens and Christmas

At the beginning of the nineteenth century, Christmas was barely celebrated and 25 December was largely seen as a normal working day, as it is for Martha Cratchit who has to work on Christmas morning. As such, Scrooge's reluctance to give Bob Cratchit the day off would not have been seen as quite as ridiculous as it is to a modern reader.

Although it would be an overstatement to claim that Dickens was responsible for 'inventing' the modern idea of Christmas, it is fair to say that the author popularised the festive season like no one before him.

The Ghost of Christmas Present dressed in green and sitting on a throne of an array of luxurious food combines the modern idea of Santa Claus with an earlier pagan figure. He symbolises Christmas ideals of warmth, feasting and decoration. Dickens's vision of Christmas is largely a secular one. Although Christian beliefs underpin the story in the references to church going — the bell in the church tower 'always peeping slily down at Scrooge' (p. 14) and the church clock which chimes out the hours in the waiting for the spirits — Dickens depicts Christmas as a joyous holiday with parties and gatherings of friends and family, rather than a sombre holy day. His love of Christmas is well documented and clearly reflected in his description of the party games, good food and mulled wine at Fred's house in Stave 3. Yet at the same time, Dickens was acutely aware of the fact that not everyone could enjoy such celebrations, as is shown in his description of the more modest Christmas enjoyed by the Cratchit family in Stave 3.

What is common to both Fred and Bob's celebration is the emphasis on the importance of friends and family. Bob is devastated when he believes that Martha may not be coming home for Christmas, and Fred makes strenuous efforts to persuade his Uncle Scrooge to join his party.

Even our modern view of the perfect Christmas being a white one is to some degree down to Dickens, probably due to the fact that his own childhood in the 1810s included several snowy Christmases. Throughout *A Christmas Carol* there are references to the wintry weather, from the snowy roofs of the houses in Stave 3 to the icy slide that Bob enjoys in Stave 1. Further discussion of the importance of Christmas can be found in the Themes section of this guide.

Dickens and the supernatural

Although the Victorian era is often associated with advances in science and technology, many Victorians remained fascinated by the supernatural and the occult. A renewed interest in spiritualism had spread to England from America. The reading public loved ghost stories, fairy tales, and Gothic tales of vampires and reanimated corpses, as in Mary Shelley's Gothic tale, *Frankenstein*.

Dickens's friend and biographer John Forster described him as having 'a hankering after ghosts', and certainly Dickens, a genius at creating sinister atmospheres, was intrigued by the supernatural, and knew there was nothing like an eerie spine-chilling tale to boost circulation for the magazines which published his works.

However, Dickens himself remained sceptical. It has been noted that he often tried to include a possible rational explanation in his supernatural writings, preferring to suggest psychological or physiological causes for ghostly phenomena. After all, the ghost of Jacob Marley which haunts the terrified Scrooge in *A Christmas Carol* could be seen as the voice of Scrooge's conscience and may have been due to a nightmare brought on by mere indigestion.

Dickens presents the reader with an interesting range of spirits in *A Christmas Carol*, and goes far beyond the conventional ghosts of Victorian literature. The ghost of Jacob Marley combines humour and horror with its clanking chains and collapsing jaw contrasted with Scrooge's often sceptical comments. The three spirits who visit Scrooge could not be more different: the child-like Ghost of Christmas Past, seeming to

Key quotation

'God bless us everyone!' said Tiny Tim. (p. 55)

Key quotation

'You may be an undigested bit of beef, a blot of mustard, a crumb of cheese, a fragment of underdone potato. There's more of gravy than the grave about you...' (p. 20)

symbolise the shifting nature of memories; the giant Ghost of Christmas Present, representing plenty, but also revealing the darker side of Christmas, hiding Ignorance and Want beneath his robe; and the terrifying Ghost of Christmas Yet to Come, a faceless, silent phantom representing our worst fears of the future.

Within 5 weeks of Dickens's death on 9 June 1870, spiritualists in America were claiming the last laugh. The spirit of the credulous sceptic had been in touch, they insisted, and had dictated various messages through raps and knocks including the ending to his unfinished last book, *The Mystery of Edwin Drood*.

REVIEW YOUR LEARNING

1 What is meant by the term 'context'?

2 Which event in his own childhood gave Dickens sympathy for poor children?

3 How might *A Christmas Carol* be seen as both a novel of social realism and a fairy tale?

4 What happened to you in Victorian times if you were unable to support yourself?

5 Why was London so overcrowded in the middle of the nineteenth century?

6 What, for Dickens, is the main way to escape poverty?

7 How is Dickens's love of the family Christmas reflected in *A Christmas Carol*?

8 Which of the ghosts in the novel is a forerunner of the modern Father Christmas?

9 What do you understand by the term 'Urban Gothic'?

10 Which nineteenth-century thinker coined the phrase 'surplus population'?

Answers on p. 99.

GRADE *FOCUS*

Grade 5
To achieve grade 5, students will show a clear understanding of the context in which the novel was written.

Grade 8
To achieve grade 8, students will make perceptive, critical comments about the ways that contextual factors affect the choices that the writer makes.

Plot and structure

Target your thinking

- What are the main events of the novel? (**AO1**)
- How do these events unfold, stave by stave? (**AO1, AO2**)
- How does Dickens use structure in the telling of his tale? (**AO2**)

Plot

The novel is divided into five staves, an old fashioned word for musical stanzas or verses, appropriately enough, since the title of the novel is *A Christmas Carol*.

Stave 1: Marley's Ghost

- It is London on Christmas Eve, 7 years since his late business partner Jacob Marley died when we meet Ebenezer Scrooge, a wealthy miser.
- Scrooge works in his counting house with his ill-treated clerk, Bob Cratchit.
- His nephew, Fred, invites him to Christmas dinner but Scrooge refuses.
- Scrooge is then visited by two gentlemen who are collecting money for the poor.
- Scrooge refuses to donate to the charity and tells the men to leave.
- He chases off a young carol singer.
- Scrooge grudgingly allows Bob to have Christmas Day off.
- When he returns home, Scrooge is visited by the ghost of Marley, who tells him he will be visited by three spirits.

Stave 1 opens with the words 'Marley was dead: to begin with' (p. 7) an eerie opening line which grabs the reader's attention and introduces a sombre note. This is almost immediately dispelled by the playful, comic tone of the narrator, who comments jokingly on his own use of the simile 'as dead as a doornail'.

We are then introduced to Ebenezer Scrooge through a vivid description of his physical appearance, closely linked to his cold-hearted, tight-fisted nature.

We learn that Jacob Marley, who was Scrooge's business partner, died exactly 7 years earlier, it is Christmas Eve 'of all the good days in the year' (p. 9), and it is bitterly cold, thus creating a sense of anticipation in the reader. We also learn that Scrooge works in a counting house or accountant's office with his badly treated clerk, Bob Cratchit.

A series of visits follows, the first of which is by Scrooge's nephew, Fred, who is portrayed as a cheerful, good-humoured young man, who invites his uncle to dine with him and his wife on Christmas Day. Dickens uses Fred to present the case for Christmas as 'a kind, forgiving, charitable, pleasant time' (p. 11). Scrooge, however, refuses the invitation, clearly establishing that he despises Christmas and those who celebrate it.

Scrooge is then visited by two gentlemen charity workers who ask for a donation to help the poor at Christmas. He refuses to contribute, saying that he already helps the poor by supporting prisons and workhouses through taxes. A young carol singer flees in terror as he chases him from the door with a ruler.

Scrooge allows Bob Cratchit to have Christmas Day as a holiday, although he insists he come to work earlier on Boxing Day to make up for it. Thus Dickens demonstrates Scrooge's miserly lack of joy, compassion and warmth in every aspect of his life: as a family member, an employer and a member of his community.

Bob's excitement as he 'pelts' home to spend the evening playing blindman's-buff with his family, is contrasted with Scrooge's 'melancholy dinner in a melancholy tavern' (p. 15), after which Scrooge goes home alone.

▲ The visit of Marley's ghost

The theme of the supernatural is introduced by a series of odd occurrences which Scrooge attempts to dismiss, for example the mysterious transformation of his door knocker into the face of his late partner, Jacob Marley. These events are followed by the visit of the ghost of Marley. The ghost is weighed down by an enormous chain made of cash boxes and padlocks which he forged in life and is now obliged to drag around.

Marley's ghost tells Scrooge that he will be visited by three more spirits who will offer Scrooge an opportunity to escape the fate of Marley. The spirit leaves by the open window, joining a number of mournful phantoms, some of whom were known to Scrooge when alive. Each one is in chains, and they are all distressed at their lost power to interfere for good in human matters. Scrooge retires to bed and instantly falls asleep.

Build critical skills

How does Dickens prepare the reader throughout Stave 1 for the visit by Jacob Marley?

Stave 2: The First of the Three Spirits

- At 1 a.m. Scrooge is visited by the child-like Ghost of Christmas Past.
- The spirit takes Scrooge back to his lonely schooldays.
- Scrooge witnesses the kindness of his late sister, Fan, the mother of his nephew, Fred.
- Scrooge is shown himself as an apprentice to Mr Fezziwig and reminded of his wonderful Christmas parties.
- Scrooge is forced to witness the ending of his engagement to Belle because of his love of money.
- He is then shown that Belle now has a husband and children.
- Scrooge cannot bear to see more and struggles with the spirit to put out its light.

When the clock strikes one, Scrooge is visited by the Ghost of Christmas Past, a child-like spirit which emits brilliant light, a light which is used to illuminate both Scrooge's personal history and the folly of his ways. This spirit, who appears to represent the theme of memories, takes Scrooge to witness scenes from his earlier life.

Key quotation

A solitary child, neglected by his friends, is left there still. (p. 31)

We first see Scrooge as a neglected schoolboy whose only friends seem to be the characters in the books he reads, thus showing the reader that Scrooge was not always the unfeeling person we were introduced to in Stave 1 and offering some explanation of his solitary nature.

He weeps in pity for the lonely schoolboy he once was. Later we see him with his younger sister, Fan, who has come to bring him home for the holidays. The ghost points out that his sister had a 'large heart' (p. 35). She has died, but the ghost prompts Scrooge to reveal that her son is his nephew, Fred, making Scrooge feel 'uneasy in his mind' (p. 35) as he has earlier treated Fred with disdain and refused Fred's offer to join him to celebrate Christmas.

Next we are shown Scrooge as a young apprentice working for Mr Fezziwig. On Christmas Eve, Mr Fezziwig tells Scrooge and his other apprentice, Dick Wilkins, to make the warehouse ready for a party. His excitement and good humour is very different from Scrooge's grumpiness towards Bob in the preceding stave. Everyone is welcome at Mr Fezziwig's ball, and the young Scrooge has a wonderful time. The ghost appears to play devil's advocate, telling Scrooge that Fezziwig has done nothing special, only spent a little money he can easily afford to make others happy. Scrooge's spirited defence of his former employer and his words, 'I should like to be able to say a word or two to my clerk just now' (p. 39), suggest the pricking of his conscience at the contrast between himself and Fezziwig's treatment of him as a clerk.

Next, the reader sees Belle, Scrooge's ex-fiancée. Belle releases Scrooge from his engagement to her because she can see that he no longer loves her as money has taken over his life.

The ghost then shows Scrooge Belle's life some years later. She now has a husband and children and, although they are not as rich as Scrooge, they are happy. They are presented as an idealised tableau of family life, offering a powerful contrast to Scrooge's lonely bachelorhood.

Scrooge cannot bear to see any more and struggles with the spirit, attempting to put out its light by forcing the extinguisher-cap over its head, as if he can no longer bear the pain of further self-knowledge.

Stave 3: The Second of the Three Spirits

- Scrooge is visited by the Ghost of Christmas Present.
- After touring the festive streets, the spirit shows Scrooge how the Cratchit family celebrates Christmas.
- Scrooge sees the frail Tiny Tim and asks if the boy will live.
- Scrooge is reminded of his earlier cruel words about the poor.
- The ghost briefly shows Scrooge how other poor people celebrate.
- Scrooge is taken to the party at his nephew Fred's house.
- Two dirty children are seen under the ghost's robe — Ignorance and Want.
- The last of the spirits appears and moves towards Scrooge.

Scrooge awakes as the clock strikes one. Seeing a ghostly light in the adjoining room, Scrooge enters and meets his next ghostly visitor: the Ghost of Christmas Present. The spirit is a giant figure in a green robe trimmed with fur and carrying a torch shaped like 'Plenty's horn' (p. 46). He has transformed Scrooge's room, in which there is now a roaring fire, filling it with piles of festive food and drink. The spirit appears to represent 'plenty', something that Scrooge has never seen the like of before.

▲ 'He seized the extinguisher-cap, and by a sudden action pressed it down upon its head.'

19

▲ The Ghost of Christmas Present

Touching the spirit's robe, Scrooge is taken on a tour of the city streets on Christmas morning and is shown that despite the 'gloomy' sky (p. 47) and icy conditions there is an 'air of cheerfulness' (p. 48) abroad. Dickens then vividly describes the shops and their wares, emphasising the joys of the festive season, and Scrooge notes that the spirit sprinkles incense from his torch to improve both the flavour of food and the mood of the people of the city.

The spirit then takes Scrooge to the 'four-roomed house' (p. 51) of his clerk Bob Cratchit and reveals to him how the Cratchit family, despite their poverty, celebrate Christmas. As Scrooge looks on, the reader is introduced to the family and Dickens shows them to be happy despite their poverty, Mrs Cratchit and her daughter both being described as 'brave in ribbons' (p. 51). The Cratchits may be seen to represent the 'dignified poor' and the importance they place on family is clearly shown in their greeting of the arrival of Bob, carrying Tiny Tim upon his shoulders.

Bob Cratchit has six children, the youngest being the frail Tiny Tim. After witnessing their modest Christmas 'feast' of goose and Christmas pudding, Scrooge asks the spirit if Tiny Tim will live, but the spirit tells him that, unless there are changes in the future, the boy will die. When Scrooge protests, the spirit reminds him of his earlier callous words to the charity collectors in Stave 1.

Key quotation

'If he be like to die, he had better do it, and decrease the surplus population.' (p. 55)

Scrooge's feelings of guilt are increased when he witnesses the family toast him as 'The founder of the Feast' (p. 56) despite Mrs Cratchit's reluctance to do so, describing Scrooge as an 'odious, stingy, hard, unfeeling man' (p. 56).

After briefly showing Scrooge a family of miners, two lighthouse keepers and some sailors on a ship, all celebrating Christmas, the spirit takes Scrooge to witness the party at his nephew Fred's house.

Fred reveals that he believes Scrooge should be pitied not despised, but his guests still enjoy a parlour game in which Scrooge is described as 'a disagreeable animal' (p. 64).

Dickens perhaps reveals his weakness for young pretty women in the rather lascivious description of Scrooge's niece as having 'a ripe little mouth, that seemed made to be kissed' (p. 60) and in his amusement at Topper's pursuit of the 'plump sister' (p. 63).

Near the end of the stave, the spirit begins to age. Scrooge sees, under the ghost's robe, two horrible and dirty children who, the spirit informs him, belong to Man. Scrooge is told that the boy is 'Ignorance' and the girl is 'Want', and to 'beware them both' (p. 67) but most of all the boy. When Scrooge asks if they can be helped, his words from Stave 1 come back to haunt him once more: 'Are there no prisons?...Are there no workhouses?' (p. 67).

As the bell strikes 12, the ghost disappears and the last of the spirits comes 'like a mist along the ground, towards him' (p. 67).

Stave 4: The Last of the Spirits

- The final spirit is the faceless Ghost of Christmas Yet to Come.
- Scrooge is shown a group of businessmen discussing an unpopular person's death.
- He then witnesses a pawnbroker buying a dead man's property.
- The scene changes to a darkened room containing only a corpse upon a bed.
- At the Cratchit house the family are mourning the death of Tiny Tim.
- Scrooge is taken to an overgrown graveyard and sees his own gravestone.
- Scrooge promises he will change his ways.

The final spirit is the menacing figure of the Ghost of Christmas Yet to Come. It is a faceless, hooded phantom which points but does not speak and is 'shrouded in a deep black garment...' (p. 67). Of all the spirits in *A Christmas Carol* Dickens presents this one as the most terrifying, representing as it does the future that awaits Scrooge if he does not change his ways. In many ways, it resembles the popular image of the Grim Reaper.

The spirit first takes Scrooge to the business centre of London and shows him a group of heartless businessmen, callously discussing someone who has recently died. This person seems very unpopular as it appears that no one intends to attend his funeral. Although Scrooge appears unaware of who is being discussed, it is clear to the reader that Scrooge himself is the topic of the conversation.

Build critical skills

Why do you think Dickens shows the reader and Scrooge the way that Christmas is spent by the miners, the lighthouse keepers and the sailors?

Key quotation

'It's likely to be a very cheap funeral,' said the same speaker; 'for upon my life I don't know of anyone to go to it.' (p. 69)

Next, the spirit accompanies Scrooge to 'an obscure part of the town' (p. 71) and Dickens juxtaposes the wealthy business region of the city with an unpleasant area of poverty and deprivation.

Scrooge is now shown a pawnbroker, old Joe, who is buying property from a laundrywoman called Mrs Dilber, a cleaner, and an undertaker's assistant. These people have taken items from a dead man, including sheets, towels and the curtains from his bed. This would have been particularly shocking for Victorian readers as the Victorians held the rites and rituals of death as sacred. Even old Joe appears shocked that the dead man's bedclothes and curtains have been taken. Once again, it is made clear that the dead man has died friendless and uncared for.

This group, like the businessmen, illustrate the outcome of a life where profit comes before all else. They are perhaps no better nor worse than their outwardly more respectable counterparts.

There follows a frightening interlude where Scrooge finds himself alone in the darkness with the body of the dead man who is 'unwatched, unwept, uncared for' (p. 75). Scrooge asks to see some 'emotion caused by this man's death' (p. 76). He is shown a young couple who owed the man money. The wife (Caroline) fears they are ruined but her husband says there is hope now their creditor is dead. The debt will be transferred to someone else, but no one else could be as 'merciless' (p. 77) as the man who has died. Caroline is described as 'mild and patient' (p. 77) but even she is presented as 'thankful in her soul' (p. 77) to hear of the man's death.

Scrooge desires to see some 'tenderness connected with a death' (p. 77) and now returns with the ghost to Bob Cratchit's house. The family are very quiet and obviously in mourning for Tiny Tim. Bob comes home after visiting the green place where Tiny Tim will be buried and goes to sit with his son, who has clearly only just died. The warmth with which Tiny Tim is remembered by his family provides a powerful contrast to the coldness and lack of compassion shown toward the unnamed dead man earlier in the stave.

At this point, Scrooge still does not realise the true identity of the dead man, even after looking in at the window of his own office and seeing that 'the figure in the chair was not himself' (p. 81).

Finally, the spirit takes him to a churchyard 'overrun by grass and weeds' (p. 81), and here Scrooge sees his own name on a neglected gravestone and realises the truth. Scrooge begs the spirit to tell him whether the things he has seen are what will be or what may be. He falls to his knees and promises that he will change his ways.

Stave 5

- Scrooge wakes up transformed to find it is Christmas Day.
- He sends a boy to buy a turkey for the Cratchit family.
- Scrooge makes a large donation to the charity collectors.
- He visits his nephew and enjoys the dinner and party.
- On Boxing Day he tells Bob he will raise his salary.
- Scrooge becomes a 'second father' to Tiny Tim.
- The final line repeats Tiny Tim's words 'God bless Us, Every One!'

When Scrooge wakes up next morning, the reader is presented with a transformed man, giddy with happiness. He feels 'quite a baby' (p. 84) suggesting he has been reborn as a result of the night's events. Dickens places the 'new Scrooge' into situations which mirror events in the opening stave of the novel so that we can clearly see the huge difference in his actions caused by his redemption.

▲ Scrooge sees his own gravestone

Promising to change his ways and delighted to find his bed-curtains not torn down, Scrooge wonders how much time has passed while he was with the spirits, and calls to a boy from his window to ask what day it is. The boy tells him it is Christmas Day. Scrooge sends the boy to the poulterer to purchase the prize turkey, which he intends to send to Bob Cratchit as an anonymous gift. Dickens stresses Scrooge's new found generosity with his offer of half a crown to the boy for his troubles and his insistence on paying for a cab to take the turkey to Camden Town.

In the street, a smiling Scrooge meets one of the charity collectors he had angrily sent away in the opening stave. He whispers to him, clearly promising to give a great deal of money to the charity. Scrooge explains that his donation includes 'a great many back-payments' (p. 86).

After going to church, Scrooge goes to his nephew Fred's house where he is greeted warmly and thoroughly enjoys the dinner and the party.

On Boxing Day, Scrooge arrives early at the office and plays a trick on Bob, pretending to be angry with him for being so late for work. He tells

Key quotation

Wonderful party, wonderful games, wonderful unanimity, won-der-ful happiness! (p. 88)

Bob that he will not 'stand for this sort of thing any longer' (p. 88) as if he is about to sack him. He then tells Bob, who thinks Scrooge has gone mad and is considering calling for a 'strait-waistcoat' (p. 88), that he is going to raise his salary. Scrooge tells him to put more coal on the fire, a demand which emphasises Scrooge's new-found warmth, and promises that he will try to help Bob's 'struggling family' (p. 89).

Dickens ends the story by telling the reader how Scrooge totally changes his outlook on life and becomes known as a man who knows how to celebrate Christmas.

Scrooge also becomes a 'second father' to Tiny Tim, 'who did not die' (p. 89), and the novel's final line repeats Tiny Tim's Christmas blessing: 'God bless Us, Every One!'

GRADE BOOSTER

Turn to p. 95 of the Top ten section for ten short, memorable quotations on the key moments in Scrooge's transformation. You will find this useful as a short summary of what happens to him.

The structure of the novel

A Christmas Carol is tightly structured. The first and last staves act as 'bookends' around the central staves, each of which is devoted to the visit of a spirit. It is symmetrical since Scrooge meets the same visitors as in Stave 1, and the novel begins and ends in the same place, Scrooge's office, but with a central protagonist who is completely transformed from the character who was presented to us in Stave 1.

Another way of looking at the structure is to consider it in terms of exposition, rising action, climax and denouement. Stave 1 provides the exposition, where the action is located in a time and place and some background information is given on the central protagonist, Ebenezer Scrooge.

The instigator is in this case Jacob Marley, who sets the tale in motion with his warning about the necessity to change and his prediction that three spirits will visit Scrooge.

The three central staves deal with the visits of the three spirits and form the rising action which climaxes with the vision of Scrooge's tombstone. This is followed by the final stave which forms the denouement when the story's loose ends are tied up and matters are resolved.

GRADE *BOOSTER*

Usually, the examination question will explain briefly where in the novel the extract is taken from. It won't necessarily tell you what happens just before or just after the extract. You don't *need* to know, but when writing about plot and structure, it can be helpful to know. For example, you may be able to refer to the use of contrast with other events, foreshadowing or dramatic irony. So make sure you have a really clear grasp of the order of events.

REVIEW YOUR LEARNING

1   What is the essential information in Stave 1 which forms the exposition?

2   List the three different visitors who come to Scrooge's door.

3   What is Marley's role in the novel?

4   Why do you think Dickens shows us Scrooge as a schoolboy?

5   Why is Scrooge upset by the sight of Belle's beautiful daughter?

6   Which family represents the dignified poor?

7   What are the names of the two children shown to Scrooge by the Ghost of Christmas Present?

8   Whose name does Scrooge find on a tombstone in a neglected graveyard?

9   How does Dickens use structure and contrast to highlight the loneliness of Scrooge's death?

10 In what sense might the novel be described as symmetrical in structure?

Answers on p. 99.

Characterisation

Target your thinking

- Who are the key characters in the novel? (**AO1**)
- How does Dickens make his characters come to life? (**AO2**)
- What purposes are served by the characters? (**AO1, AO2**)
- Do the characters have symbolic value? (**AO1, AO2, AO3**)

Dickens uses a variety of techniques to present the characters in *A Christmas Carol* to the readers:

- Description of the character including appearance, body language and setting.
- The life circumstances and actions of the character.
- What the character says.
- What other characters say about them.
- The intrusive comments of the narrator.
- The development or otherwise of the character.

Scrooge

The presentation of the character of Scrooge embodies the concept of change since he alters twice in the course of the novel, from the lonely schoolboy revealed by the Ghost of Christmas Past to the miser we meet in Stave 1, and then again to the transformed Scrooge in the final stave.

GRADE *BOOSTER*

Always remember that the characters in the novel have been created by a writer and that your focus needs to be on the ways that the writer has made the characters come alive for the reader. Don't write about the characters as if they were real people. If the words 'Dickens' or 'the writer' don't appear several times in your answer you are probably not answering the question and you are unlikely to achieve high marks.

The Scrooge of popular culture is most clearly shown in Stave 1 when presented by Dickens as **cold-hearted**, through exaggerated physical description, suggesting that he is frozen inside and that this has affected his appearance.

His lack of empathy towards the poor is confirmed by the words: 'Are there no workhouses?' as well as the description of his ill treatment of Bob whom he threatens to sack merely for applauding Fred.

His most famous characteristic is his **miserly nature** and this is clearly established by Dickens through a range of methods, beginning with the use of a list of adjectives, 'a squeezing, wrenching, grasping, scraping, clutching, covetous old sinner' (p. 8) which creates a strong impression of a man determined to hang on to every last penny.

The description of his shocking refusal to give money to the charity collectors and his chasing the carol singer further develop this idea. The boy is 'gnawed' with cold, making Scrooge seem like a particularly nasty bully. Further evidence of meanness is seen through his unreasonable reluctance to give the likeable Bob the whole day off on Christmas day.

Key quotation

'A poor excuse for picking a man's pocket every twenty-fifth of December…But I suppose you must have the whole day.' (p. 15)

His meanness is also the reason for his preference for the dark.

Key quotation

Darkness is cheap and Scrooge liked it. (p. 17)

Dickens uses humour to present Scrooge's **dislike of Christmas**, when Scrooge declares that '…every idiot who goes about with "Merry Christmas" on his lips should be boiled with his own pudding, and buried with a stake of holly through his heart' (p. 10) and also through the catchphrase 'Bah! Humbug!'.

However, he begins to change when visiting the past. His memories move him to emotion and seeing the world beyond his office, home and tavern with the Spirit of Christmas Present also affects him, as does encountering the shocking reality of Ignorance and Want beneath the festive facade.

His transformation is complete after witnessing the circumstances of his 'death' and seeing his own lonely, neglected grave.

In the final stave we see a Scrooge who is **no longer emotionally frozen** as he whoops with joy at his rebirth and laughs with sheer relief and delight.

Dickens uses contrast with Stave 1 to show how generous he has become through his purchase of the turkey for Bob, as well as the promise of a raise, his tipping of the boy, and the donation to the charity collectors which contains a 'great many back-payments' (p. 86).

Build critical skills

The cold within him froze his old features, nipped his pointed nose, shrivelled his cheek, stiffened his gait; made his eyes red, his thin lips blue; and spoke out shrewdly in his grating voice. (p. 8)

How has Dickens made this description of Scrooge effective for the reader?

Build critical skills

'I don't know anything. I'm quite a baby. Never mind. I don't care. I'd rather be a baby. Hello! Whoop! Hallo here!' (p. 84)

How does this extract, where the language is quite different from his previous speech, deepen your understanding of Scrooge's state of mind?

Build critical skills

When Bob Cratchit leaves Scrooge's office, Dickens describes him as going down a slide 'twenty times, in honour of its being Christmas Eve' (p. 15) and then running home to play blindman's buff.

How do these details add to our understanding of Bob's character? Do you think this behaviour is typical of an adult after a hard day at work?

comforter: a woollen scarf

He now appears as sociable as he was previously isolated. Dickens describes his walk through the streets, patting children on the head, his attendance at Fred's party and his joking with Bob, who presumes Scrooge has gone mad!

He becomes an utterly changed man and 'a second father' (p. 89) to Tiny Tim.

Key quotation

...he knew how to keep Christmas well, if any man alive possessed the knowledge. (p. 89)

Bob Cratchit

Bob Cratchit, Scrooge's over-worked and under-paid clerk, represents the dignified poor as well as symbolising the true spirit of Christmas. A kind, caring man with a large family to support, Bob is introduced in Stave 1 in direct contrast to Scrooge's cold, miserly ways and dislike of the festive season.

Bob is initially presented by Dickens almost as a prisoner, working in a cold and 'dismal little cell' (p. 9) highlighting the poor working conditions endured by workers at that time. The colour of Bob's white comforter perhaps hints at his innocence and goodness.

Dickens shows Bob to have a warm heart. He applauds Fred's spirited defence of Christmas, even at the risk of losing his job, returns Fred's seasonal greetings 'cordially' and is not discouraged by the grudging and graceless manner of Scrooge. Despite the extreme cold, he has 'no great coat', and readers soon begin to feel sympathetic towards this downtrodden but cheery worker.

Dickens suggests Bob's love for his family as he arrives from church with Tiny Tim on his shoulders, through his praise of his wife's cooking and also through his devastated reaction when he thinks that his daughter Martha may not be home for Christmas.

Key quotation

'Not coming!...Not coming upon Christmas Day!' (p. 52)

Bob shows physical warmth towards his family as he hugs Martha and sits close to Tiny Tim and holds his 'withered little hand' (p. 55).

▲ '...and in came little Bob, the father,... and Tiny Tim upon his shoulder.'

His happy family life is presented as another contrast to Scrooge's isolation. The meagre but jolly Cratchit 'feast' is compared to Scrooge's 'melancholy dinner'.

Dickens's description of Bob serving the hot gin punch 'with beaming looks, while the chestnuts on the fire sputtered and cracked noisily' (p. 55) represents an idealised version of a traditional Christmas scene.

Dickens shows us a man who, unlike his wife, does not bear a grudge through his toasting of Scrooge as 'the Founder of the Feast' (p.56). He acts as a moral compass for the family as he gently guides his wife to take a more charitable view.

His quiet dignity is shown when grieving for the loss of Tiny Tim. Dickens refers to him as 'little Bob' (p.79). His small stature may be connected with a lack of nourishment, but might also suggest that he has been somewhat diminished by Tim's tragic 'death'.

He shows no self-pity, appreciating the kind words offered by Fred. His faith and spirituality are expressed in the lines, '"I am very happy," said little Bob, "I am very happy!"' (p. 80).

Build critical skills

It is clear in Stave 5 that Bob forgives Scrooge, as he allows Scrooge to become a 'second father' (p. 89) to Tiny Tim.

How do you react to Bob's conduct as he mourns the death of his son?

Mrs Cratchit

Although only appearing in Staves 3 and 4, Bob's wife still makes an impact on the reader, and Dickens presents her as a good wife and mother who makes the best of difficult circumstances.

Mrs Cratchit is portrayed as a loving wife, describing her husband as 'precious' (p. 51), but she also appears as a lively woman who joins in with the joke against Bob when pretending Martha is not coming home for Christmas. She is clearly proud of being able to put a decent meal on the table at Christmas despite the family's poverty. She is only ever seen indoors as 'The Angel in the House' (the title of a narrative poem about an ideal marriage by Coventry Patmore's (1823–96), and embodies the traditional Victorian views of womanhood. Her chief concern is for her family, as she warmly welcomes Martha as she comes in from work, and for the pudding, as she had doubts about the 'quantity of flour' (p. 54).

Mrs Cratchit does not, however, seem to share her husband's forgiving nature as she recoils at the idea of toasting the health of Mr Scrooge, describing him as 'an odious, stingy, hard, unfeeling man' (p. 56).

Build critical skills

...Bob, turning up his cuffs — as if, poor fellow, they were capable of being made more shabby... (p. 53)

What do we learn about Bob through Dickens's descriptions of his clothing?

Build critical skills

Despite Bob's efforts to put on a brave face, how does Dickens suggest Bob's feelings about Tiny Tim in the following lines?

Bob's voice was tremulous when he told them this, and trembled more when he said that Tiny Tim was growing strong and hearty. (p. 53)

Build critical skills

...Mrs. Cratchit, Cratchit's wife, dressed out but poorly in a twice turned gown, but brave in ribbons, which are cheap and make a goodly show for sixpence... (p. 51)

What does Dickens's choice of tone and detail suggest about the character and voice of Mrs Cratchit in this quotation?

Key quotation

'...*I wouldn't show weak eyes to your father when he comes home, for the world.'* (p. 78)

Nevertheless, Dickens shows that, as an obedient wife, she complies with Bob's request and grudgingly drinks Scrooge's health.

In Stave 4, Dickens presents Mrs Cratchit as a picture of domesticity, sewing by the fire with her daughters as one of the boys reads from the Bible. She is, however, emotionally strong, putting on a brave face after Tiny Tim's 'death' and supporting her husband in his grief.

Belle

Belle, who appears only in Stave 2, is a young woman who Scrooge once loved. In her first appearance she is in mourning dress, and there are tears in her eyes. This creates immediate sympathy for her, and as the tears sparkle in the light from the Ghost of Christmas Past she is linked with the goodness and purity of that spirit.

With a heavy heart, she releases Scrooge from his engagement to her because she believes he has replaced her with a 'golden' idol, recalling biblical images of false gods, and again emphasising her goodness. Dickens presents her using all the stereotypical Victorian feminine virtues. She is 'fair' and she speaks 'softly' and 'gently' and wishes him well as he leaves, without any anger or bitterness. 'May you be happy in the life you have chosen!' (p. 41).

Later in the stave we see that she has married and this time she is presented as a perfect wife and mother, laughing heartily and enjoying the noise and 'tumultuous' behaviour of her many children. She is now 'a comely matron' (p. 41) with a beautiful daughter. She represents Scrooge's lost chance of happiness, and the sight of her with her husband and daughter is so painful to Scrooge that he begs the spirit to take him away.

Belle and Caroline, another 'mild and patient creature' (p. 77), are both further examples of the perfect 'sweet, submissive and domesticated' woman Patmore portrayed in his poem 'The Angel in the House', which opens with the words:

'Man must be pleased: but him to please

Is woman's pleasure.'

The Cratchit children

Martha is the oldest of the Cratchit children, 'a poor apprentice at a milliner's' (p. 57). Martha's late arrival is due to having to work on Christmas Day. Her love of her family is suggested through her involvement in the joke played on Bob and her reluctance to 'see him disappointed' (p. 52).

Belinda is the second daughter, described as, 'brave in ribbons' (p. 51) like her mother. She is shown helping her mother by laying the cloth, sweetening the apple sauce, and changing the plates.

Peter is the oldest son, who wears his father's hand-me-down shirt and considers the possibility of earning 'five-and-sixpence weekly' to be 'bewildering' (pp. 56–57).

Two Young Cratchits — these are a lively unnamed boy and girl who 'danced about the table' (p. 51) in their excitement over Christmas.

Tiny Tim is the angelic, invalid, youngest child who has 'his limbs supported by an iron frame' (p. 52) and who offers the toast of 'God bless Us Every One!' (p. 55).

▲ The Cratchit family may be seen to represent the 'dignified poor'

Marley's ghost

Although only appearing in Stave 1, the Ghost of Jacob Marley plays an important role in the novel, preparing the reader for much of the later action. One of the purposes of Marley's ghost is to create a supernatural atmosphere in the opening stave, which Dickens achieves with his opening line: 'Marley was dead: to begin with', and by revealing that Marley has died, '...seven years ago, this very night...' (p. 12).

In terms of the plot, Marley's ghost simply serves to prepare Scrooge (and the reader) for the visit of the three spirits, but his visit to Scrooge also introduces some key themes of the novel. Marley's ghost is wrapped in a huge chain made up of 'cash-boxes, keys, padlocks, ledgers, deeds and heavy purses' (p. 19) as a reminder of his obsession with business when he was alive, and this, of course, serves to warn Scrooge that his actions on earth will affect him after his death. This image also recalls some of the medieval paintings with which Dickens would have been familiar, where the damned were shown with objects that symbolised the sins they had committed on earth. The Victorians were obsessed with death and what might happen after it. Visions of hell and fears of eternal punishment overshadowed many Victorian lives.

Dickens makes it clear that Marley's ghost regrets his behaviour on earth and his failure to see that there are more important things than money and business.

It might be argued that Dickens's presentation of Marley's ghost, with its clanking chains, transparent body and 'frightful cry' (p. 21) is the most conventional spirit in the novel.

Key quotation

'I am here to-night to warn you, that you have yet a chance and hope of escaping my fate.' (p. 24)

Build critical skills

'Why did I walk through crowds of fellow-beings with my eyes turned down...' (p. 23)

How do Marley's words serve to remind the reader of Scrooge?

Fred

Fred is Scrooge's nephew, the son of his late sister, Fan, and Scrooge's only surviving family member. Although sometimes seen as a minor character in the novel, it is interesting to note that Fred appears (or is referred to) in every stave. Indeed, some critics have noted Fred, with his love of Christmas and his warm and compassionate nature, to be Dickens's mouthpiece in *A Christmas Carol*.

Fred's appearance in Stave 1 is clearly meant to provide a stark contrast to Scrooge's cold, miserly nature. Fred sees Christmas as a '...kind, forgiving, charitable, pleasant time...' (p. 11), four adjectives that could not be applied to Scrooge and his actions in this stave.

Despite Scrooge's refusal to accept his invitation to Christmas dinner, Fred maintains his good humour. His forgiving nature is shown once again in Stave 3 when he says of Scrooge to his guests that he '...couldn't be angry with him if [he] tried...' (p. 61).

Dickens, as the third-person intrusive narrator, draws particular attention to Fred's laugh.

Key quotation

'Ha, ha! laughed Scrooge's nephew. 'Ha, ha, ha!'

If you should happen, by any unlikely chance, to know a man more blessed in a laugh than Scrooge's nephew, all I can say is, I should like to know him too. Introduce him to me, and I'll cultivate his acquaintance. (p. 60)

Fred's warmth and compassion is further suggested in Stave 4 when he offers his condolences and help to Bob Cratchit and is described by him as 'the pleasantest-spoken gentleman you ever heard' (p. 79) and in Stave 5 when he warmly greets his uncle's arrival: 'Let him in! It is a mercy he didn't shake his arm off' (p. 88).

The Ghosts of Christmas Past, Christmas Present and Christmas Yet to Come

The three spirits obviously play a huge role in the transformation of Scrooge, each one showing him the error of his ways. However, each ghost is presented in a highly individual way by Dickens.

The Ghost of Christmas Past

This spirit is perhaps the most unusual of the three. Dickens describes the ghost as being 'like a child' (p. 28) yet at the same time seeming like an old man. The ghost appears to represent memory, which might be of long past events or loved ones, but memories can, at the same time, seem new and fresh in the hearts and minds of those who remember. Its strong hands might suggest the powerful hold that the past can sometimes exert on the present. Furthermore, the figure is said to have 'fluctuated in its distinctness' (p. 29), perhaps suggesting the sometimes indistinct nature of memories.

Build critical skills

…from the crown of its head there sprung a bright clear jet of light… (p. 28)
What do you think this light might represent?

The purpose of this spirit is two-fold: to reveal aspects of Scrooge's past to the reader, showing us, for example, the lonely schoolboy he once was and revealing that as a young man Scrooge still enjoyed the festivities of Christmas; and also to begin to open Scrooge's eyes to the error of his ways by creating guilt in him for his harsh treatment of both his employee Bob and his ex-fiancée Belle, who was cast aside due to Scrooge's love of money. The link with light is an interesting one as Victorian readers would associate the light with goodness and with Christ in particular, who was referred to in the Bible, as 'the light of the world'. For further discussion on the symbolic importance of light in the novel, turn to the Themes section under the heading 'Light and dark' on p. 45.

Build critical skills

'…the only time I know of,…when men and women seem by one consent to open their shut-up hearts freely, and to think of people below them as if they really were fellow-passengers to the grave…' (p. 11)

How does Fred's view of Christmas contrast with his Uncle Scrooge's?

Build critical skills

'Come in! and know me better, man!' (p. 46)

How do you interpret the spirit's words, particularly his use of the word 'man'?

The Ghost of Christmas Present

The second spirit, a jolly giant dressed in green and white, is presented surrounded by festive food, in front of a roaring fire and carrying a torch '...not unlike Plenty's horn...' (p. 46). Thus he is immediately linked with food and warmth. His antique scabbard, which is empty, suggests peace on earth and his 'open hand' is contrasted with Scrooge's tight fist in Stave 1.

The Ghost accompanies Scrooge through the city streets on Christmas morning, sprinkling good cheer from his torch, and on to the Cratchits' home where Scrooge witnesses their modest but warm-hearted family celebrations. After this, Scrooge is taken to see Christmas among miners, lighthousemen and sailors who all find ways to celebrate the season despite their poverty and isolation. Scrooge's final destination with the Ghost of Christmas Present is Fred's house, where Scrooge is shown the party games being played, sometimes at his expense.

Build critical skills

Why do you think Dickens presents the figures of Want and Ignorance in the folds of the spirit's robes?

Although this ghost appears good natured, Dickens also uses him for a more serious purpose. First, the ghost reminds Scrooge of his earlier callous comments about the 'surplus population' (p. 55) and then, as he ages, he reveals the horrifying figures of Want and Ignorance who lurk beneath his robes.

The Ghost of Christmas Yet to Come

The final spirit is a more conventional ghost, a terrifying faceless phantom which, unlike the other ghosts, does not speak. It communicates with Scrooge only through its 'out-stretched hand' (p. 67) and frightens Scrooge more than any of the ghosts he has encountered so far.

Build critical skills

The Phantom slowly, gravely, silently approached... (p. 67)

It was shrouded in a deep black garment, which concealed its head, its face, its form... (p. 67)

How does Dickens present the Ghost as a terrifying and mysterious figure in these two quotations? Think particularly of the effect of the words 'gravely' and 'shrouded'.

The Ghost takes Scrooge to the financial centre of the City where he overhears two groups of wealthy businessmen discussing an unpopular man who has recently died. While it is clear to the reader who the subject of these conversations is, Scrooge remains in the dark.

The Ghost also serves to reveal the horrific effects of poverty when taking Scrooge to 'an obscure part of the town' (p. 71) where Scrooge witnesses three characters selling the belongings of a dead man to the pawnbroker, old Joe.

The Ghost's final purpose in Stave 4 is, of course, to force Scrooge to see his eventual fate by revealing to him the 'neglected grave' (p. 82) marked by his name.

REVIEW YOUR LEARNING

1 Why does Scrooge threaten to sack Bob Cratchit?

2 What technique does Dickens use to emphasise Scrooge's miserly nature in his introduction of him as a character?

3 Why does Scrooge like darkness?

4 What might Bob Cratchit be said to represent?

5 What phrase does Dickens use to present Bob as a prisoner?

6 What is the significance of the chain worn by Marley's ghost?

7 Which character might be seen as a mouthpiece for Dickens's own views about Christmas?

8 What purpose is served in the novel by the Ghost of Christmas Past?

9 How does Dickens show the darker side of Christmas through the otherwise jolly Ghost of Christmas Present?

10 In what ways might the Ghost of Christmas Yet to Come be described as a more 'conventional' ghost?

Answers on p. 100.

GRADE FOCUS

Grade 5

To achieve grade 5, students will develop a clear understanding of how and why Dickens uses language, form and structure to create characters, supported by appropriate references to the text.

Grade 8

To achieve grade 8, students will examine and evaluate the ways that Dickens uses language, form and structure to create characters, supported by carefully chosen and well-integrated references to the text.

Themes

Target your thinking

- What is a theme? (**AO1, AO3**)
- What are the main themes in *A Christmas Carol*? (**AO1, AO3**)
- Why are themes so important in *A Christmas Carol*? (**AO1, AO3**)
- What is a motif? (**AO1, AO3**)
- What are the motifs that occur in *A Christmas Carol*? (**AO1, AO3**)

In literature, a theme is an idea that a writer explores through the plot, structure, characters and descriptions in the novel. It is usually something that the writer wants you, the reader, to think about. In some instances, writers may hope that as a result of thinking about a particular theme, the reader may reconsider their attitudes and even their behaviour. Although Dickens was addressing the problems of a particular time and place, it can be argued that his themes have universality, which means that many of his concerns are still relevant to us today.

There are some critics, such as E. M. Forster, who feel that many of Dickens's characters are rather one-dimensional. Forster states: 'Dickens's people are nearly all flat.' In *A Christmas Carol* the reason that this is so may be because, for Dickens, the messages he wanted to convey were what was really important to him. These messages are expressed through the themes of the novel. This is part of the sense for many, such as the critic Grace Moore, that the novel could be considered an allegory of redemption, where characters represent particular vices, virtues or a group within society, such as Bob Cratchit representing all industrious, down-trodden workers.

There are several different ways of categorising these themes, and in any interpretation of literary themes, there is bound to be some overlap. Here is a suggested list of how the main themes of *A Christmas Carol* might be grouped:

- poverty
- isolation
- the importance of family
- the meaning of Christmas

Poverty

Dickens himself was deeply concerned by the plight of the poor and was involved with a number of charities, and this is reflected in his exploration of the theme of poverty. He uses the character of Scrooge to exemplify the callous attitude of the more affluent to the underprivileged in Victorian society. This is shown through Scrooge's attitude to the request for a donation from the charity collectors and the husband of Caroline's description of Scrooge as 'so merciless a creditor' (p. 77) when the couple cannot but rejoice in his death. Many Victorians lived in fear of ruin because of debt; see p. 8 in the Context section for Dickens's own experience of debt as he was growing up, an experience he was never to forget.

Bob Cratchit is employed by Dickens to symbolise the typically exploited worker at the mercy of his tyrannical employer. He toils for low pay in a cold office, while his daughter Martha, a poor apprentice at a milliner's, has to work on Christmas morning and only just gets home in time for Christmas dinner.

Dickens uses a somewhat sentimental portrayal of the Cratchit family to represent the respectable, hard-working poor. Bob has no great coat and his threadbare clothes are 'darned up and brushed to look seasonable' (p. 52) while his wife is 'dressed out but poorly in a twice-turned gown' (p. 51). His son Peter wears a hand-me-down shirt from Bob but 'rejoiced to find himself so gallantly attired' (p. 51). They do not complain about their situation or the meagre nature of their feast and would have been ashamed to be thought ungrateful. This links to a Christian belief in the virtue of patiently enduring poverty without complaint, though there is also a sense that in such a loving family these good-natured children would never be so churlish as to hurt their parents' feelings by any suggestion that what was provided was insufficient.

At a time when the infant mortality rate among the poor was very high, the 'death' of Tiny Tim represents the fate of the many sick children living in poverty. These children were, in Scrooge's view, part of the 'surplus population' who would be better off dead. However, the reality of his thoughtless words is revealed to him when he actually spends some time watching Tim and the family.

Tiny Tim is one of a number of sick or dying children in Dickens's novels, the most famous of whom is probably Little Nell in *The Old Curiosity Shop*. Oscar Wilde, a playwright and great wit of the period, is attributed with having once said: 'One must have a heart of stone to read the death of Little Nell without laughing!' However, most Victorians would have been moved by Tim's plight, as there was a general tendency in literature and art to sentimentalise children and in particular, childhood illness and death.

Build critical skills

Caroline is anxious for the return of her husband and his face is 'careworn and depressed' (p. 77). She is glad to hear of the death of Scrooge, although she immediately repents her instinctive response. Even their children, though they do not fully understand the situation, are happier. What does this suggest to the reader about the effect of debt on decent people?

Key quotation

...nobody said or thought it was at all a small pudding for a large family. It would have been flat heresy to do so. (p. 54)

Dickens goes on to further explore the darker side of poverty through the description of the two hideous children of Man, Ignorance and Want, who lurk beneath the gown of the Ghost of Christmas Present. The ghost's statement that of the two, Ignorance is worse, reflects Dickens passionately held belief that only with education can the cycle of poverty be broken. Scrooge's words, which are thrown back at him by the spirit, 'Are there no workhouses?' (p. 67) drive home the message that the wealthy are selfish and uncaring, especially in the light of Tiny Tim's probable death.

▲ Ignorance and Want — 'They are Man's,' said the Spirit, looking down upon them.

The outcome of Ignorance and Want can be found in the 'den of infamous resort' (p. 71), a part of town which Scrooge has never visited, thus emphasising the gulf between the rich and the poor. It is here that the sordid reality of deprivation is revealed within the chaos and filth of old Joe's shop. It is here that the charwoman, the laundress and the undertaker's assistant meet to try and get a few coins in exchange for Scrooge's belongings.

Despite his views on the shocking plight of the impoverished working class, there is no suggestion in *A Christmas Carol* that Dickens was in any way a revolutionary in the same way as Marx and Engels, who were revolutionary political theorists of the time. They shared Dickens concerns, over for example the way that workers were treated by the factory and mine owners. However, they believed in direct action, i.e. that the workers should unite and completely change the system. They should own the factories themselves and demand better working conditions, more money and greater social equality, rather than relying on charity.

Dickens's solution, on the other hand, was spiritual and philanthropic. He appears to be suggesting that employers should, like the Fezziwigs, treat their employees more kindly and fairly, and that those with wealth should be generous with charitable aid and show greater empathy to those who are struggling.

Isolation

The theme of isolation is explored through the presentation of Scrooge. It is introduced in the first stave with a striking simile which tells us he was as 'secret, and self-contained, and solitary as an oyster' (p. 8). This suggests that he has a hard exterior, and that, like an oyster, it is difficult to get him to open up in order to find the 'pearl' of goodness inside.

Dickens goes on to explain that he actively avoids all human contact, apparently having driven everyone away from him. The repetition of the word 'no' at the start of each clause in the key quotation on the right helps to drive the message home.

We then see his refusal to spend Christmas with Fred (an idea which is presented as quite shocking), his dismissal of the charity collectors and his chasing of the carol singer as he leaves to spend Christmas Eve alone, taking 'his melancholy dinner at his usual melancholy tavern' (p.15) in the company of his newspapers and his banker's book.

His isolation extends to his home as he lives in a building where he is the only inhabitant as the other rooms are all let out as offices. This means that he has no community or local network to support him. Even the building itself is out of the way, 'up a yard where it had so little business to be, that one could scarcely help fancying it must have run in there when it was a young house, playing hide-and-seek with other houses, and forgotten the way out again' (p. 16).

The character of Jacob Marley is also used to warn both Scrooge and the reader of the perils of isolating oneself from one's community.

Key quotation

No beggars implored him to bestow a trifle, no children asked him what it was o'clock, no man or woman ever once in all his life inquired the way to such and such a place, of Scrooge. (p. 8)

Key quotation

'It is required of every man,' the Ghost returned, 'that the spirit within him should walk abroad among his fellowmen, and travel far and wide; and if that spirit goes not forth in life, it is condemned to do so after death.' (p. 21)

Key quotation

'This is the end of it, you see! He frightened every one away from him when he was alive, to profit us when he was dead! Ha, ha, ha!' (p. 75)

It is only when Scrooge visits his own past that we discover that isolation may be all that he knows, and we therefore begin to see him in a slightly more sympathetic light. We see for example, Scrooge as 'a solitary child, neglected by his friends' (p. 31). He is alone in a 'long, bare, melancholy room' (p. 32), the repetition of the word 'melancholy' perhaps offering a clue as to why Scrooge was drawn to the 'melancholy tavern' to take his supper alone.

Unlike the adult Scrooge, the child is described as 'lonely' rather than just solitary. He comforts himself with imaginary characters from his story books which become his friends. We learn that Scrooge has spent other Christmases shut away from his family in the over-strict school and that his father appears to have been cruel towards him.

Towards the end of the novel, we see the terrifying spectacle of his unloved corpse lying on a bed in the dark, stripped of any dignity by the theft of his possessions which are haggled over by old Joe and the grotesque trio of Mrs Dilber, the charwoman and the undertaker's

Scrooge with Bob: '"...I am about to raise your salary!"' ▶

assistant. This is ironic, since his isolation in life has led to the invasion of his house and the violation of his corpse. The Victorians believed strongly in respect for the dead and so the attitude of the three scavengers would have been particularly shocking.

His business associates and men 'of great importance' (p. 70) appear quite indifferent to his demise, despite Scrooge having 'made a point always of standing well in their esteem' (p. 70).

In the final stave, we see a Scrooge who no longer desires isolation. He walks among humankind, never having dreamed that a walk could make him so happy. Finally, he visits his nephew Fred, where he has a wonderful time.

His recovery appears complete when we see him actually touching another human being on the following day, when he jokes with Bob, poking him in the ribs and clapping him on the back (p. 89).

Build critical skills

He went to church, and walked about the streets, and watched the people hurrying to and fro, and patted children on the head, and questioned beggars, and looked down into the kitchens of houses, and up to the windows, and found that everything could yield him pleasure. (p. 87)

Look carefully at the verbs in this sentence. How does Dickens show Scrooge's gradual reintegration into society?

The importance of family

In *A Christmas Carol*, happiness is equated with being part of a family. The only kindness that Scrooge seems to have known as a child is connected with his sister, Little Fan, who comes to him one year to take him home from school. His connection to Fan is represented by her surviving son, Fred, who persists in inviting 'Uncle Scrooge' to dinner, presumably because of the family connection. Scrooge's bitterness about love and marriage is expressed in his rejection of Fred's invitation and his mockery of the fact that Fred, unlike Scrooge, married for love. Perhaps Scrooge's rejection of Fred is also connected to the idea that Fred reminds him that he too could have had a happy marriage, instead of being a miserable old bachelor.

The first idealised vision of family life is shown in the description of his lost love Belle and her husband and children. Scrooge witnesses Belle as a 'comely matron' (p. 41) with her daughter, a beautiful young girl. Both are smiling happily amidst domestic chaos and more lively young children than Scrooge could count. The children rush to the door in excited anticipation as their father returns home, and it is clear that the sight of their enthusiastic affection is painful to Scrooge, since he knows that he threw away the opportunity to become Belle's husband and father to her children.

Key quotation

And now Scrooge looked on more attentively than ever, when the master of the house, having his daughter leaning fondly on him, sat down with her and her mother at his own fireside; and when he thought that such another creature, quite as graceful and as full of promise, might have called him father, and been a spring-time in the haggard winter of his life, his sight grew very dim indeed. (pp. 42–43)

Dickens reinforces the point when this delightful tableau is contrasted with the husband's reported sighting of Scrooge in his office, 'quite alone in the world' (p. 43).

The Cratchits too are used to suggest that a happy family life without much money is preferable to a prosperous, single life. The Cratchits are a highly sentimentalised portrait of a working-class family. Despite the stress of their economic situation and Tim's ill health, they do not appear to complain, quarrel or fight among themselves.

Key quotation

...they were not well dressed; their shoes were far from being water-proof; their clothes were scanty; and Peter might have known, and very likely did, the inside of a pawnbroker's. But they were happy, grateful, pleased with one another, and contented with the time...' (p. 57)

Marriage and family are presented as a source of support as the Cratchits help each other deal with their grief when Tiny Tim 'dies', Caroline and her husband share their relief at Scrooge's death and even when the miners sing together in their hut on the moor.

Key quotation

So surely as they raised their voices, the old man got quite blithe and loud; and as surely as they stopped, his vigour sank again. (p. 59)

Scrooge is only happy when he reconnects with Fred and becomes a second father to Tiny Tim.

The meaning of Christmas

Key quotation

'...a few of us are endeavouring to raise a fund to buy the Poor some meat and drink, and means of warmth. We choose this time, because it is a time, of all others, when Want is keenly felt, and Abundance rejoices.' (p. 13)

Although the backdrop of *A Christmas Carol* is clearly a Christian festival and moral values underpin the novel in the shape of kindness, generosity and care for others, there is little sense of solemn religious ceremony in the novel. In fact, when Scrooge questions the Ghost of Christmas Present about the movement to close the baker's on Sundays and holidays, the spirit denies all responsibility, stating that those who wish to deprive the poor of the means of cooking dinner on the seventh day, are 'strange' to him, and that they act out of 'passion, pride, ill-will, hatred, envy, bigotry, and selfishness' (p. 50). For Dickens, Christmas is about celebration: family gatherings, parties, food, drink and music. Those who enjoy these benefits should be generous to their neighbours and give charity to those in need.

The theme of family is closely related to that of Christmas, since happiness at Christmas seems to equate primarily with the warmth and love of a family Christmas.

Key quotation

There all the children of the house were running out into the snow to meet their married sisters, brothers, cousins, uncles, aunts, and be the first to greet them. (p. 57)

Dickens describes actual family gatherings, like the Cratchits or the miners, but also includes wider celebrations which may have family at their heart, such as the Fezziwigs's Christmas dance or Fred's Christmas party.

Food and music are key elements that bring people together in the festive season, no matter what their situation, economic status or the class to which they belong. We see this first at the Fezziwigs, where the abundance of food on offer illustrates the generous nature of Scrooge's first employer.

Key quotation

…there was cake, and there was negus, and there was a great piece of Cold Roast, and there was a great piece of Cold Boiled, and there were mince pies, and plenty of beer. (p. 37)

negus: a drink made from wine, sugar, water, lemon juice and nutmeg

The Ghost of Christmas Present symbolises plenty as he sits upon a throne of festive fayre consisting of several types of meat, cakes and fruit, which Dickens presents in a long list to emphasise the abundance of good things. Dickens's readers would have been amazed at the description of such a fantastical amount of food in one place, as Victorian homes did not have refrigeration.

The markets are also described in sensual detail and with something approaching rapture when it comes to the grocer's shop.

Build critical skills

It was not alone that…the blended scents of tea and coffee were so grateful to the nose, or even that the raisins were so plentiful and rare, the almonds so extremely white, the sticks of cinnamon so long and straight, the other spices so delicious, the candied fruits so caked and spotted with molten sugar as to make the coldest lookers-on feel faint and subsequently bilious. Nor was it that the figs were moist and pulpy, or that the French plums blushed in modest tartness from their highly decorated boxes… (p. 49)

How has Dickens made the above description of Christmas produce so effective? Choose three examples and analyse in detail both the methods used and the effects on the reader.

At the Cratchits', however, a small goose had to be 'eked out with apple-sauce and mashed potatoes' (p. 54) but, like the pudding, was still a cause of great excitement.

GRADE *BOOSTER*

Examination questions may ask you to consider how Dickens uses a particular character to present a theme. For example, how does Dickens present the theme of Christmas through the Ghost of Christmas Present? Learn to think of characters in this way.

Key quotation

…the two young Cratchits…crammed spoons into their mouths, lest they should shriek for goose before their turn came to be helped. (p. 53)

smoking bishop: a punch made from port and red wine, sugar, spices and oranges or lemons

There was also plenty of alcohol involved in a Dickensian Christmas. The goose was washed down by some hot mixture in a jug with gin and lemons. Over at Fred's they drank hot mulled wine, and when Scrooge relented towards Bob, he promised to discuss the help Scrooge will give Bob over 'a Christmas bowl of smoking bishop' (p. 89).

Music is another important ingredient in the celebration of Christmas. It is used to symbolise the joy of the season, from the carol singer in Stave 1 to the Fezziwigs's Christmas party, where a fiddler accompanies the dancing, to the lighthouse keeper who sings 'a sturdy song' (p. 59) and to the old miner, who sings a very old Christmas song to the three generations of his family who are gathered around him. Even the watchman on the ship 'hummed a Christmas tune' (p. 59). The noise of the people scraping the snow off the pavements in front of their house makes 'a rough, but brisk and not unpleasant kind of music' (p. 47).

At the Cratchits', Tiny Tim sings a song 'about a lost child travelling in the snow' (p. 57) and at Fred's, Scrooge's niece plays a tune on the harp which had been familiar to Little Fan and as Scrooge listens to it he 'softened more and more' (p. 62) and began to wonder if he might have been a kinder man if he had listened to the tune more often.

No wonder then that Dickens decided to call his seasonal tale, *A Christmas Carol*.

Finally, Christmas is also presented as a time for adults to re-engage with their 'inner child'.

GRADE **BOOSTER**

Turn to p.93 of the Top ten section for short memorable quotations on the main themes. You will find it useful to have them at your fingertips in the examination.

Key quotation

After a while they played forfeits; for it is good to be children sometimes, and never better than at Christmas… (p. 63)

Key quotation

There might have been twenty people there, young and old, but they all played, and so did Scrooge. (p. 64)

More than anything for Dickens, the holiday is about having fun. Jokes are all part of it, from the prank that Mrs Cratchit and Martha play on Bob, the laughter and merriment at Fred's party and the joke that Scrooge plays with such delight on Bob when he pretends to be angry about Bob's lateness.

Snowballs are pelted by the city folk as they shovel and scrape snow and Bob Cratchit can be seen going 20 times down a slide on Christmas Eve and racing home to play blind-man's buff with his children. The same game is played at Fred's where it affords Topper the opportunity for a little seasonal flirting with the plump sister, and they also play forfeits, 'How, When and Where' and various other parlour games.

Motifs

A motif is an idea or object that recurs throughout a literary work. It is different from a theme which is a central idea, but it may be used to enhance our understanding of other themes and ideas. The main motifs which can be found in *A Christmas Carol* are:

- time
- light and dark
- cold and heat

Time

Time is referred to on a number of occasions in the novel. For example, it is significant that it is 7 years since Marley died and that the story is set at Christmas, a very particular time of the year. The ghosts are differentiated by their relationship to time: Past, Present and Christmas Yet to Come. Marley tells Scrooge he will be visited on three consecutive nights but at the end of the story Scrooge is overjoyed to discover that time has been manipulated and magically the 'Spirits have done it all in one night' (p. 84).

Time is made concrete by the many references to clocks and chimes, beginning with the church tower in Stave 1.

Key quotation

The ancient tower of a church, whose gruff old bell was always peeping slily down at Scrooge out of a Gothic window in the wall, became invisible, and struck the hours and quarters in the clouds, with tremulous vibrations afterwards as if its teeth were chattering in its frozen head up there. (p. 14)

The Spirits arrive on the tolling of the hour bell, and in the final stave Scrooge was 'checked in his transports by the churches ringing out the lustiest peals he had ever heard' (p. 84). The doleful and portentous striking of the clock during the night is replaced by this joyfulness.

Light and dark

The story begins on a day which was quite dark already, and this helps to create the sombre atmosphere of Scrooge's Christmas, which appears to grow darker as he approaches his home. We are told that he likes darkness because it was cheap, but the physical darkness might also be used to symbolise the darkness of his soul as well as the darkness of ignorance in which he lives.

Build critical skills

The Spirit stood beside sick beds, and they were cheerful; on foreign lands, and they were close at home; by struggling men, and they were patient in their greater hope; by poverty and it was rich. In almshouse, hospital and jail, in misery's every refuge, where vain man in his brief little authority had not made fast the door, and barred the spirit out, he left his blessing and taught Scrooge his precepts. (p. 65)

What do you think is Dickens's message about the power of the spirit of Christmas?

Build critical skills

'I will live in the Past, the Present, and the Future!' Scrooge repeated, as he scrambled out of bed. 'The spirits of all Three shall strive within me.' (p. 83)

What do you think Scrooge means by this? What might Dickens's message be?

On the other hand, the opening of Stave 5 and the first day of the transformed Scrooge is marked by 'clear, bright' weather and 'Golden sunlight!' (p. 84). Furthermore, it is noticeable that the first two spirits are linked with light, the Ghost of Christmas Past with its 'bright clear jet of light' (p. 28) illuminating Scrooge's past, and the Ghost of Christmas Present turning Scrooge's room into a glade of 'bright gleaming berries' which 'reflected back the light' (p. 45).

Cold and heat

The contrast of cold and heat as a motif is also interesting. In Stave 1, Scrooge is described in terms of being cold from the inside out.

However, Fred is described in terms of external warmth suggesting the warmth of his personality.

Scrooge's office and home are both poorly heated, and Marley's 'death-cold eyes' exert a 'chilling influence' (p. 19) on Scrooge. Belle and her daughter, on the other hand, sit in comfort next to the 'winter fire' (p. 41). The Ghost of Christmas Present appears in front of 'a mighty blaze...roaring up the chimney' (pp. 45–46) and on their tour of the town on Christmas Eve, every house is 'expecting company, and piling its fires half-chimney high' (p. 58), thus linking warmth with happiness and hospitality.

However, it is clear that cold weather is not in itself a cause for misery. In Stave 1, Dickens describes the foggy weather as 'piercing, searching, biting, cold' (p. 14) and the nose of the poor carol singer as 'gnawed and mumbled by the hungry cold as bones are gnawed by dogs' (p. 14). Yet, in Stave 5, when the mist has cleared, Scrooge experiences 'bright, jovial, stirring, cold; cold, piping for the blood to dance to' (p. 84). Perhaps Dickens is thinking back to the happy, snowy Christmases of his early childhood.

REVIEW YOUR LEARNING

1 What is a theme?

2 How is a theme different from a motif?

3 What are the main themes in *A Christmas Carol*?

4 What was Dickens's purpose in exploring the theme of poverty?

5 What is the simile that Dickens uses to describe Scrooge which introduces the theme of isolation?

6 How does Dickens present the theme of family life?

7 What does Dickens see as the main elements of a happy Christmas?

8 What are the main motifs in *A Christmas Carol*?

9 How are Scrooge's office and home similar?

10 What might Scrooge's love of darkness symbolise?

Answers on p. 100.

GRADE *FOCUS*

Grade 5

To achieve grade 5, students will reveal a clear understanding of the key themes of the novel and how Dickens uses language, form and structure to explore them, supported by appropriate references to the text.

Grade 8

To achieve grade 8, students will be able to examine and evaluate the key themes of the novel, analysing the ways that Dickens uses language, form and structure to explore them. Comments will be supported by carefully chosen and well-integrated references to the text.

Language, style and analysis

Target your thinking

- How does Dickens reveal the story of *A Christmas Carol* to his readers? (**AO2**)
- What are some of Dickens's more typical language techniques? (**AO2**)
- How does Dickens create atmospheric settings in the novel? (**AO2**)

You will notice from the questions above that when analysing language and style, the Assessment Objective with which we are most concerned is AO2, which refers to the writer's methods and is usually highlighted in the exam question by the word 'how'. It is of vital importance since it is the means by which writers help to create our understanding of plot, character and themes.

Examiners report that AO2 is often the most overlooked by students in the examination. For example, candidates who fail to address AO2 often write about the characters in a novel as if they were real people involved in real events rather than analysing them as 'constructs' or creations of the writer.

To succeed with AO2, you must deal effectively with the writer's use of language, form and structure. Turn to p. 24 for analysis of the structure of *A Christmas Carol*.

Form

The form of the novel refers to the choice that the writer makes in terms of how he/she tells the story, in other words, the viewpoint. For example, Dickens could have written the story in the first person. In that case, Scrooge himself could have related the story of how his life was transformed by what happened to him on the night he was visited by Spirits. This method is sometimes used to allow the reader to become closer to the main character.

This approach can create sympathy, understanding and affection for a central protagonist. However, it also means that the events are told through only one pair of eyes, potentially leading to biased or unreliable narration. The reader does not have access to all of the events in the novel or the innermost feelings of other characters, unless the first-person storyteller does.

Instead, Dickens chose to write the novel in the third person, using the device of the Spirits and their capacity for time travel to allow Scrooge to see events that he would be unable to see in a story that was more firmly rooted in realism.

The third person is often used to create the illusion of an observer who is detached from the action, rather than part of it. For example, 'Scrooge never painted out Marley's name' (p. 8) or 'The clerk observed that it was only once a year' (p. 15).

However, in the case of *A Christmas Carol*, we are also aware of the presence of a narrator, who, from time to time, intervenes in the story with jokes, exclamations and direct address to the reader. For example, at the very beginning of the story he comments on his own use of the simile, 'dead as a doornail' (p. 7), and when the Ghost of Christmas Present takes Scrooge to view Scrooge's nephew's party, the narrator says of Fred: 'If you should happen, by any unlikely chance, to know a man more blest in a laugh than Scrooge's nephew, all I can say is, I should like to know him too' (p. 60). This method is often referred to as the third-person intrusive form. It creates a more intimate relationship between the narrator and the reader.

The narrator, who appears at times to be both erudite in his cultural references and witty in his remarks, can only be assumed to be Dickens himself. We know that he toured both in England and America reading his story aloud to adoring fans. He was said to be a talented, witty and dramatic performer, and clearly enjoyed the effect on the audience created by these knowing asides. Readers too will often have a sense of his particular voice and personality at certain points in the novel.

'Form' can also be used more generally to describe the genre or kind of novel that the writer has written. For further discussion on the genre of the novel, turn to p. 69 in the section on Assessment Objectives.

Dickens's use of language

One way of thinking about Dickens's use of language is to imagine the novel as a gigantic Christmas cake stuffed with sultanas, currants, almonds, raisins, candied peel, walnuts and cherries, each of which represents a Dickensian language feature. Imagery, syntax, symbolism, contrast and humour are just some of the methods used in order to present serious messages in an entertaining but thought-provoking way.

Imagery

One of Dickens's most distinctive features is his mastery of imagery which he employs in various ways throughout the novel in order to create a range of effects.

For example, **similes** are used effectively on numerous occasions. Scrooge, we are told, is 'hard and sharp as flint' (p. 8) creating the impression of someone without any feelings. Since flint is a very hard substance, the suggestion is that he is a person who would be very

simile: a comparison using the words 'as' or 'like'

uncomfortable to be around. Likewise, simile is used when the pudding emerges from the copper at the Cratchits'. The smell is at first 'like a washing day' (p. 54) and then 'like an eating-house and a pastrycook's next door to each other, with a laundress's next door to that!' (p. 54). The care with which Dickens uses precise detail to evoke the particular smell in this instance is what makes this description so vivid and appealing to the senses.

Simile is also used by Scrooge to describe his ecstatic state in Stave 5: 'I am as light as a feather, I am as happy as an angel, I am as merry as a schoolboy. I am as giddy as a drunken man' (p. 83). Here, Scrooge's simple joy is reflected by the simplicity of the language.

> **metaphor:** a comparison which doesn't use 'like' or 'as' but instead says something is something else

Dickens also uses powerful **metaphors**. In Stave 1, he evokes the misery of Bob's life as a wage slave when he tells us that he works in a 'cell'. The supernatural events that are to come later in the story are subtly **foreshadowed** through metaphor when he describes the houses in the fog as 'mere phantoms' (p. 9).

> **foreshadowing:** a technique used to warn the reader of a future event

Elsewhere, metaphor is used by Dickens to sharply refute Malthusian sentiments when the Ghost of Christmas Present rebukes Scrooge for his thoughtless comments on surplus population.

Key quotation

'Oh God! to hear the Insect on the leaf pronouncing on the too much life among his hungry brothers in the dust!' (p. 56)

Build critical skills

A frosty rime was on his head, and on his eyebrows, and his wiry chin. (p. 8)

Why do you think Dickens chose to use this metaphor to describe both Scrooge's appearance and his character?

Scrooge is by pure chance an insect 'on the leaf' with plenty of food. The image shows how small the individual is in the grander scheme of things, and stresses that Scrooge does not have the right to decide whether the less fortunate 'in the dust' (p. 56) should live or die.

A type of metaphor of which Dickens is very fond is **personification**. For example, in Stave 1 he creates the idea of the cold as malevolent. 'The water plug, being left in solitude, its overflowing sullenly congealed, and turned to misanthropic ice' (p. 14).

> **personification:** when an abstract idea or inanimate object is given human characteristics

A particularly effective image is that of the nose of the young carol singer which was 'gnawed and mumbled by the hungry cold as bones are gnawed by dogs' (p. 14). This suggests a cold that is so vicious and relentless that it causes pain as it eats away at the young and vulnerable.

The personification used to describe the fruiterers adds to the impression of a scene bursting with life, for example, in the description of the Spanish onions: '...ruddy, brown-faced, broad-girthed Spanish Onions, shining in the fatness of their growth like Spanish Friars, and winking from their shelves in wanton slyness at the girls as they went by...' (p. 48), an image which manages to combine a sense of the shape and colour of the onions with both holiness and a kind of jocular naughtiness, perhaps reminiscent of the increased licence of the season.

Repetition

Dickens often uses repetition for emphasis, but also for its sonorous rhythmical effect. For instance, the following statement combines negative repetition and hyperbole with alliteration to express Scrooge's inner coldness. It perhaps needs to be read out loud to fully appreciate its musicality.

Key quotation

No warmth could warm, no wintry weather chill him. No wind that blew was bitterer than he, no falling snow was more intent upon its purpose, no pelting rain less open to entreaty. (p. 8)

Humour

There are many examples of humour in *A Christmas Carol*. Sometimes Dickens uses visual humour, for example, Scrooge's confusion in trying to get dressed in Stave 5, when he makes 'a perfect Laocoön of himself with his stockings' (p. 83).

He also uses puns or word play, when for example, Scrooge tells Marley's ghost that he is more 'gravy' than 'grave' (p. 20) and when he puns on the word 'spirits' with the idea of alcoholic spirits at the end of the novel — 'He had no further intercourse with Spirits, but lived upon the Total Abstinence Principle ever afterwards' (p. 89).

He also uses understatement or litotes in a drily humorous manner to signify Scrooge's complete lack of emotion at Marley's death: 'And even Scrooge was not so dreadfully cut up by the sad event, but that he was an excellent man of business on the day of the funeral, and solemnised it with an undoubted bargain' (p. 7).

On the other hand, in Scrooge's Christmas message to Fred, exaggeration or hyperbole is also used for comic effect: '...every idiot who goes about with "Merry Christmas" on his lips should be boiled with his own pudding, and buried with a stake of holly through his heart' (p. 10).

Exaggeration is used in the description of Scrooge in Stave 1 and also in the caricatures of the business men, where inner ugliness is reflected in their appearances: one a 'great fat man with a monstrous chin' (p. 69) and the other 'a red-faced gentleman with a pendulous excrescence on the end of his nose, that shook like the gills of a turkey-cock' (p. 69).

Build critical skills

The chuckle with which he said this, and the chuckle with which he paid for the Turkey, and the chuckle with which he paid for the cab, and the chuckle with which he recompensed the boy, were only to be exceeded by the chuckle with which he sat down breathless in his chair again, and chuckled till he cried. (pp. 85–86)

How does Dickens use repetition in this extract and how does it affect the reader? Can you see a significant link to another character with a very infectious laugh?

Laocoön: a figure from Greek mythology who was killed by two sea serpents

syntax: grammar;
sentence construction

Build critical skills

Heaped up on the floor, to form a kind of throne, were turkeys, geese, game, poultry, brawn, great joints of meat, sucking-pigs, long wreaths of sausages, mince-pies, plum-puddings, barrels of oysters, red-hot chestnuts, cherry-cheeked apples, juicy oranges, luscious pears, immense twelfth-cakes, and seething bowls of punch, that made the chamber dim with their delicious steam. (p. 46)

What effects are created by this sentence?

Build critical skills

Characters such as Scrooge and Bob are contrasted in that Scrooge is alone, wealthy and miserable while Bob is a family man, poor but happy.

How does Dickens contrast Scrooge with Fred at the beginning of the novel?

Irony is another technique Dickens uses to create humour. There is detailed discussion of how Dickens uses irony on pp. 53–54.

GRADE BOOSTER

Make a collection of your favourite comic quotations with brief notes. Research has shown that many students find it easier to remember something that makes them laugh. You may also wish to check the Top ten section on p.91 where you will find lists of quotations on characters, themes and key moments in Scrooge's development.

Syntax

One of the first stylistic features you may have noticed is Dickens's use of long, often complex sentences to create particular effects, for example, in the use of a list of nouns in the description of the throne of gourmet food on which the Ghost of Christmas Present sits.

Rather than using a single adjective Dickens often chooses to uses lists of adjectives for emphasis. For example, while waiting for the first visit of a spirit, the momentousness of the event is signified by the sounding of the hour bell 'with a deep, dull, hollow, melancholy *One'* (p. 28).

Word order is also used to create effects, for example, in the following sentence, which describes the sunset, as Scrooge and the ghost speed towards the miners' hut: 'Down in the west the setting sun had left a streak of fiery red, which glared upon the desolation for an instant, like a sullen eye, and frowning lower, lower, lower yet, was lost in the thick gloom of darkest night' (p. 58).

The sentence seems to take the reader lower and lower, reflecting both the dying sun and the work of the miners themselves, and ending with the words 'darkest night'.

Contrast

Contrast is also used by Dickens. In Stave 1, the homes and shops of the more fortunate are bright and warm, as preparations are made for the Christmas festivities. 'The Lord Mayor, in the stronghold of the mighty Mansion House, gave orders to his fifty cooks and builders to keep Christmas as a Lord Mayor's household should...' (p. 14). This is used to counterpoint the description of the 'ragged men and boys' in front of a brazier 'warming their hands and winking their eyes before the blaze in rapture' (p. 14). Within the context of 'intense' cold, this highlights the theme of social inequality which runs throughout the novel.

In order to drive home his message at the end of Stave 4, Dickens contrasts Scrooge's corpse, which lies 'plundered and bereft, unwatched, unwept, uncared for' (p. 75) in darkness, with the body of Tiny Tim, which is in a room which is 'lighted cheerfully, and hung with Christmas' (p. 79) and visited frequently by his grieving family.

Symbolism

A Christmas Carol is rich in **symbolism** throughout, from the fog of ignorance that pervades Stave 1 to the glorious bright light of redemption in Stave 5. The chains and cashboxes that weigh Marley down may represent his guilt for the sins of greed and avarice that he committed in life. He carries them with him for all eternity.

Characters too act as symbols; for example Scrooge could be seen to symbolise all selfish business people in the same way as Tiny Tim might represent all poor and vulnerable children. The Ghost of Christmas Past may symbolise memory, the Ghost of Christmas Present embodies the warmth and generosity of the Christmas spirit, and the faceless Ghost of Christmas Yet to Come suggests the unknown future. Turn to the Characterisation section on p. 26 for more detail on characters who are also symbols.

> **symbolism:** when a word, image or character carries a wider meaning as well as its literal meaning

Irony

There are three main types of irony: dramatic, verbal and situational. In *A Christmas Carol* you will find examples of all three.

Dramatic irony

Dickens uses dramatic irony to great effect in Stave 4. This is when the reader knows something that a character or characters are not aware of. For example, Scrooge is unaware that the dead man who is being discussed is himself, while the reader has a growing sense that this is the case.

This involves the reader, as by this stage in the novel it is apparent that Scrooge is beginning to change and so his words create sympathy for him as he does not yet know the awful truth. Tension and anticipation increase as the stave builds to its horrific climax as Scrooge reads his own name on the grave in the lonely churchyard.

> **Key quotation**
>
> *'I see, I see. The case of this unhappy man might be my own.' (p. 75)*

Verbal irony

Verbal irony is when the opposite of what is meant is said. It may be used for comic effect, for example, in Dickens's comments on the flirting between Topper and the plump sister, where he feigns shock and moral outrage at Topper's behaviour: 'No doubt she told him her opinion of it, when… they were so very confidential together, behind the curtains' (p. 63).

Verbal irony is also used in the description of the neglected graveyard where Scrooge sees his tombstone. In describing it as 'A worthy place!' (p. 81), Dickens could be suggesting the exact opposite. In much the same way, he uses the term 'dainties' as part of a comic reversal of what we might expect in the reference to 'a decanter of curiously light wine and a block of curiously heavy cake' (p. 34) which the schoolmaster offers little Fan and young Scrooge.

Situational irony

Situational irony is employed when Scrooge asks to be taken to see an example of some emotion at the death of the, as yet, unknown man, and the emotion he is shown is happiness: 'We may sleep tonight with light hearts, Caroline!' (p. 77).

Description of settings

A wide range of settings are described, but perhaps the most memorable are:

- Scrooge's chambers
- old Joe's shop and its environs
- the streets outside Scrooge's office

When the story begins, the foggy weather and almost unnatural darkness — 'it had not been light all day' (p. 9) — immediately establishes a sinister tone as the reassuring normality of everyday London life is hidden from view. Dickens used fog in similar ways near the start of both *Bleak House* and *Great Expectations*. In *A Christmas Carol*, the fog is used to suggest menace and mystery. It appears all-encompassing, as it 'came pouring in at every chink and keyhole' (p. 9). Dickens uses the fog, which thickens as the day progresses, to suggest that the story is moving towards some momentous event. It could also be suggested that the fog represents Scrooge's ignorance and lack of awareness.

Dickens creates an atmosphere of icy coldness through the alliteration of words like 'bleak' and 'biting' and through emphasising the sounds of passers-by.

Key quotation

It was cold, bleak, biting weather: foggy withal: and he could hear the people in the court outside, go wheezing up and down, beating their hands upon their breasts, and stamping their feet upon the pavement stones to warm them. (p. 9)

However, in Stave 2, as Scrooge journeys through the snowy streets with the Ghost of Christmas Present, Dickens describes a scene of great cheerfulness. The people clear snow, make their way to church and carry their dinners to the bakers to be cooked, while the shops offer tantalising glimpses of their delicious produce. In Stave 5, Dickens makes use of pathetic fallacy as Scrooge rejoices in glorious wintry sunshine as the 'merry bells' (p. 84) ring out and he walks the same streets in great delight.

pathetic fallacy: when the weather or nature is used to reflect someone's feelings or mood

Scrooge's chambers

The chambers described in Stave 1 provide the setting for the visits of the spirits. Although we are told that Scrooge lived alone, there is from the beginning of the description a sense of the presence of supernatural 'others'. It is, we are told, easy to imagine the 'Genius of the Weather' watching 'in mournful meditation' at the gateway to Scrooge's building (p. 16). This seems to hint at some great sadness connected to Scrooge. Tension is further increased when Scrooge is startled to see Marley's face in the knocker 'like a bad lobster in a dark cellar' (p. 16), as well as a hearse being driven up the staircase.

Throughout the description, the idea of darkness pervades, in accordance with the conventions of ghost stories. The yard is so dark that Scrooge has to find his way by groping with his hands, and ascends the stairs with one inadequate candle.

Dickens uses simple statements regarding Scrooge's rooms: 'Sitting-room, bed-room, lumber-room' (p. 17). The sparseness of the language here is appropriate as a reflection of Scrooge's frugal lifestyle and the fact that he sits by a 'very low fire indeed' (p. 18) reminds the reader of his miserliness and maintains the gloomy atmosphere. The simplicity of the language contrasts with the sumptuousness of the language elsewhere in the novel, such as the description of the grocer's shop that is shown to Scrooge by the Ghost of Christmas Present.

Old Joe's shop

The setting of old Joe's shop offers another less romanticised view of life for the poor. It is located in a part of town where Scrooge has never been. Here, Dickens may be suggesting that those who have money are ignorant of the reality of life for those who don't. The area does not appear to accommodate the respectable poor such as the Cratchits. The inhabitants recall the wolfish children Ignorance and Want, since the people are 'half-naked, drunken, slipshod, ugly' (p. 71) and the area filthy and stinking which for the Victorians would be strongly associated with disease.

In the midst of this area is old Joe's pawnshop, and it is no less sordid than its surroundings. Dickens uses a list again, but this time the items are 'old rags', 'greasy offal' and 'rusty keys' (p. 71) to create an atmosphere of dirt and disorder as an appropriate setting for the vile business conducted there.

Build critical skills

Secrets that few would like to scrutinise were bred and hidden in mountains of unseemly rags, masses of corrupted fat, and sepulchres of bones. (p. 71)

How does this sentence add to your understanding of the setting of old Joe's shop?

GRADE *FOCUS*

Grade 5

To achieve grade 5, students will show a clear appreciation of the methods Dickens uses to create effects for the reader, supported by appropriate references to the text.

Grade 8

To achieve grade 8, students will explore and analyse the methods that Dickens uses to create effects for the reader, supported by carefully chosen and well-integrated references to the text.

REVIEW YOUR LEARNING

1 From what narrative perspective is the story of *A Christmas Carol* narrated?

2 Name two types of imagery that Dickens uses.

3 What do you understand by the term 'personification'?

4 What is meant by the term 'litotes'?

5 What do you understand by the term 'hyperbole'?

6 How does Dickens use fog in *A Christmas Carol*?

7 With what does Dickens contrast the vision of Scrooge's lonely corpse?

8 Name three important settings in the novel.

9 What technique is used when Dickens refers to the neglected graveyard as 'A worthy place!' (p. 81)?

10 What language method does Dickens use to suggest the sparseness of Scrooge's chambers?

Answers on p. 100.

Tackling the exams

Target your thinking

- What sorts of questions will you have to answer?
- What is the best way to plan your answer?
- How can you improve your grade?
- What do you have to do to achieve the highest grade?

Your response to a question on *A Christmas Carol* will be assessed in a 'closed book' English literature examination, which means that you are not allowed to take a copy of the text into the examination room. The different examination boards will test you in different ways, and it is vital that you know on which paper the nineteenth-century novel will be, so that you can be well prepared on the day of the examination.

Whichever board you are studying, the table on the following page explains which paper and section the novel appears in and gives you information about the sort of question you will face and how you will be assessed.

Marking

The marking of your responses varies according to the board your school or you have chosen. Each exam board will have a slightly different mark scheme, consisting of a ladder of levels. The marks you achieve in each part of the examination will be converted to your final overall grade. Grades are numbered from 1 to 9, with 9 being the highest.

It is important that you familiarise yourself with the relevant mark scheme(s) for your examination. After all, how can you do well unless you know exactly what is required?

Assessment Objectives for individual assessments are explained in the next section of the guide (see pp. 67–71).

Approaching the examination question

First impressions

First read the whole question and make sure you understand exactly what the task requires you to do. It is very easy in the highly pressured atmosphere of the examination room to misread a question and this can be disastrous. Under no circumstances should you try to twist the

	AQA	Edexcel	Eduqas
Paper Section	Paper 1 Section B	Paper 2 Section A	Paper 2 Section B
Type of question	Extract-based question requiring response to aspect of extract and response to the same or similar aspect in the novel as a whole.	Two-part question. Part (a) is based on an extract. Part (b) is a question asking for a response to an aspect elsewhere in the text.	Extract-based question requiring response to aspect of extract and response to the same or similar aspect in the novel as a whole.
Closed book?	Yes	Yes	Yes
Choice of question?	No	No	No
Paper and section length	Paper 1: 1 hour 45 minutes. Section B: approximately 50 minutes.	Paper 2: 2 hours 15 minutes. Section A: 55 minutes.	Paper 2: 2 hours 30 minutes. Section B: approximately 50 minutes.
% of whole grade	20% literature grade	25% literature grade	20% literature grade
AOs assessed	AO1 AO2 AO3	Part (a) AO2 Part (b) AO1	AO1 AO2 AO3
Is AO4 (SPaG) assessed in this section?	No	No	No

SPaG: spelling, punctuation and grammar

question to the one that you have spent hours revising or the one that you did brilliantly on in your mock exam.

Are you being asked to think about how a character or theme is being presented or is it a description of a place? Make sure you know so that you will be able to sustain your focus later.

Look carefully at any bullet points you are given. They are there to help and guide you.

The three boards which offer *A Christmas Carol* as a text all use an extract-based question. However, the wordings and formats of the questions are slightly different.

Have a look at this extract which could be used in a question set by any of the three boards.

They left the busy scene, and went into an obscure part of the town, where Scrooge had never penetrated before, although he recognised its situation, and its bad repute. The ways were foul and narrow; the shop and houses wretched; the people half-naked, drunken, slipshod, ugly. Alleys and archways, like so many cesspools, disgorged their offences of smell, and dirt, and life, upon the straggling streets; and the whole quarter reeked with crime, with filth, and misery.

Far in this den of infamous resort, there was a low-browed, beetling shop, below a pent-house roof, where iron, old rags, bottles, bones, and greasy offal, were bought. Upon the floor within, were piled up heaps of rusty keys, nails, chains, hinges, files, scales, weights, and refuse iron of all kinds. Secrets that few would like to scrutinise were bred and hidden in mountains of unseemly rags, masses of corrupted fat, and sepulchres of bones. (p. 71)

As a starting point, you may wish to underline keywords in the question, such as 'how' to remind you to write about methods and any other words which you feel will help you to focus on answering the question you are being asked. Below are examples of the question types from each examination board which have been annotated by students in this way.

AQA

Starting with this extract, how does Dickens present the setting of Victorian London in the novel?

Write about:

- how Dickens presents the setting of Victorian London in the extract
- how Dickens presents the setting of Victorian London in the novel as a whole   [30 marks]

Eduqas

You should use the extract and your knowledge of the whole novel to answer this question.

Write about the ways settings are described throughout the novel.

In your response you should:

- refer to the extract and the novel as a whole;
- show your understanding of the ways settings are used in the novel;
- refer to the contexts of the novel.   [40 marks]

Edexcel

(a) Explore <u>how Dickens presents</u> the <u>setting</u> of Victorian London in this extract.

Give <u>examples from the extract</u> to support your ideas.　　(20)

(b) In this extract, a powerful impression of Victorian London is created.

Explain why the <u>setting</u> is important **<u>elsewhere</u> in the novel**.

In your answer you must consider:

- <u>the different locations</u>
- <u>how important they are</u>.　　(20)

(Total for Question = 40 marks)

Spot the differences!

- AQA and Eduqas both refer to the 'whole novel'.
- Edexcel uses the phrase 'elsewhere in the novel'.
- Only Eduqas refers directly to 'contexts' in the question.
- Only Edexcel does not assess AO3 in this section.
- Only Edexcel divides the question into two separate sections, (a) and (b).

Important

All three boards assess both AO1 and AO2 in this section of the paper. Always make sure you cover both of these AOs in your response, even if they do not seem to be signposted clearly in the question.

Whichever exam board you are using, you will be required to read a passage so your next step is to read the passage very carefully, trying to get an overview or general impression of what is going on, and what or who is being described.

Working with the text

Now read the passage again, underlining or highlighting any words or short phrases that you think might be related to the focus of the question and are of special interest. For example, they might be surprising, unusual or amusing. You might have a strong emotional or analytical reaction to them or you might think that they are particularly clever or noteworthy.

These words/phrases may work together to produce a particular effect or to get you to think about a particular theme or to explore the methods the writer uses to present a character in a particular way for their own purposes. You may pick out examples of literary techniques such as lists or use of imagery, or sound effects such as alliteration or onomatopoeia. You may spot an unusual word order, sentence construction or use of punctuation. The important thing to remember is that when you start writing you must try to *explain the effects* created by these words/phrases or techniques, and not simply identify what they mean. Above all, ensure that you are answering the question.

Planning your answer

It is advisable to write a brief plan to help you to gather and organise your thoughts before you start writing your response. This will stop you repeating yourself or getting into a muddle. A plan should consist of words and short phrases — it is not a first draft. You will not have time to do this. In fact, if your plan has any full sentences, you are probably eating into the time you have available for writing a really insightful and considered answer.

You may find it helpful to use a diagram of some sort — perhaps a **spider diagram** or **flow chart**. This may help you to keep your mind open to new ideas as you plan, so that you can slot them in. You could make a list instead. The important thing is to choose a method that works for you.

If you have made a spider diagram, arranging your thoughts is a simple matter of numbering the branches in the best possible order.

The other advantage of having a plan is that if you run out of time, the examiner can look at the plan and may be able to give you an extra mark or two based on what you were going to do next.

Writing your answer

Now you are ready to start writing your answer. The first thing to remember is that you are working against the clock and so it is really important to use your time wisely.

It is possible that you may not have time to deal with all of the points you wish to make in your response. If you simply identify several language features and make a brief comment on each, you will be working at a fairly low level. The idea is to **select** the ones that you find most interesting and develop them in a sustained and detailed manner. In order to move up the levels in the mark scheme, it is important to write a lot about a little, rather than a little about a lot.

You must also remember to address the whole question as you will be penalised if you fail to do so.

If you have any time left at the end of the examination, do not waste it. Check carefully that your meaning is clear and that you have done the very best that you can. Look back at your plan and check that you have included all your best points. Is there anything else you can add? Keep thinking until you are told to put your pen down.

Referring to the author and title

You can refer to Dickens either by name (make sure you spell it correctly) or as 'the writer'. You should never use his first name (Charles) — this sounds as if you know him personally. You can also save time by giving the novel title in full the first time you refer to it, and afterwards simply referring to it as 'the novel'.

GRADE *BOOSTER*

Do not lose sight of the author in your essay. Remember that *A Christmas Carol* is a construct — the characters, their thoughts, their words, their actions have all been created by Dickens — so most of your points need to be about what Dickens might have been trying to achieve. In explaining how his message is conveyed to you, for instance through an event, something about a character, use of symbolism, personification, irony and so on, don't forget to mention his name.
For example:

- Dickens makes it clear that xxx.
- It is evident from xxx that Dickens is inviting the audience to consider xxx.
- Here, the audience may well feel that Dickens is suggesting xxx.

Writing in an appropriate style

Remember that you are expected to write in a suitable **register**. This means that you need to use an *appropriate* style. This means:

- *Not* using colloquial language or slang, e.g. 'Scrooge is a nasty piece of work. A bit of a toe-rag really.' (The only exception is when quoting from the text.)
- *Not* becoming too personal, e.g. 'Bob is like my mate, right, 'cos he...'.
- Using suitable phrases for an academic essay, e.g. 'It could be argued that', not 'I reckon that...'.
- Not being too dogmatic. Don't say 'This means that...'. It is much better to say 'This might suggest that...'.

You are also expected to be able to use a range of technical terms correctly. However, if you can't remember the correct name for a technique but can still describe it, you should still go ahead and do so.

The first person ('I')

It is perfectly appropriate to say 'I feel' or 'I think'. Just remember that you are being asked for your opinion about *what* Dickens may have been trying to convey in his novel (his themes and ideas) and *how* he does this (through characters, events, language, form and structure of the novel).

Spelling, punctuation and grammar (AO4)

Although your spelling, punctuation and grammar are **not** specifically targeted for assessment on the nineteenth-century novel, you cannot afford to forget that you will demonstrate your grasp of the novel through the way you write, so take great care with this and don't be sloppy. If the examiner cannot understand what you are trying to say, he/she will not be able to give you credit for it.

How to raise your grade

The most important advice is to answer the question which is in front of you, and you need to start doing this straight away. When writing essays in other subjects, you may have been taught to write a lengthy, elegant introduction explaining what you are about to do. You have only a short time in the Literature examination so it is best to get started as soon as you have gathered your thoughts together and made a brief plan.

Students often ask how long their answer should be. It is difficult to give a definitive answer because candidates have different sized handwriting but quality is always more important than quantity. A strongly focused answer of 2–3 pages which hits the criteria in the mark scheme will be rewarded at the very highest level. Conversely, if a response is 6–7 pages long but is not focused on the question, it will not receive many marks at all.

Sometimes students go into panic mode because they do not know how to start. It is absolutely fine to begin your response with the words, 'In this extract Dickens presents...' because whichever exam you are sitting, you need to start with the extract.

Begin by picking out interesting words and phrases and unpicking or exploring them within the context or focus of the question. For example, if the question is about the way that poverty is presented, you need to focus on picking out words and phrases to do with poverty.

What methods has the writer used? Although there are a whole range of methods with which you need to be familiar, it might be something as simple as a powerful adjective. What do you think is the impact of that word? It might be that the word you are referring to has more than one meaning. If that is the case, the examiner will be impressed if you can discuss what the word means to you, but can also suggest other meanings. Is context relevant here? In other words, would Dickens's readers view poverty differently? What might Dickens have been trying to express about poverty when he chose this word or phrase?

It is likely that you will find it easier to address AO2 (methods) when writing about the extract as you have the actual words to hand. However, do not be tempted to quote at length from the extract.

Is there an actual overall effect? For instance, you may have noticed Dickens's frequent use of lists of adjectives which create intensely vivid impressions, so as well as analysing individual words in the list (not all of them, just the most interesting ones) you could also describe the cumulative effect.

Be careful to avoid lapsing into narrative or simply retelling the story. If you are asked about how Dickens presents Scrooge, remember that the focus of the question is about the methods that Dickens uses. Do not simply tell the examiner what Scrooge does or what he is like; this is a very common mistake.

Remember you also have to deal with the focus of the question in the novel as a whole or in the case of Edexcel, 'elsewhere in the novel'. You will be penalised if you do not do this, so you MUST leave time. If you feel you have more to offer in terms of comments on the extract, leave a space so that you can return to it if necessary.

Key points to remember

- Do not just jump straight in. Spending time wisely in those first moments may gain you extra marks later.
- Write a brief plan.
- Remember to answer the question.
- Refer closely to *details* in the passage in your answer, support your comments, and remember you must also refer to the novel as a whole (or refer to 'elsewhere' in the novel for Edexcel).
- Use your time wisely. Try to leave a few minutes to look back over your work and check your spelling, punctuation and grammar, so that your meaning is clear and so that you know that have done the very best that you can.
- Keep an eye on the clock.

Grade 5 candidates

- Have a clear focus on the text and the task and are able to 'read between the lines'.
- Develop a clear understanding of the ways in which writers use language, form and structure to create effects for the readers.
- Use a range of detailed textual evidence to support comments.
- Use understanding of the idea that both writers and readers may be influenced by where, when and why a text is produced.

Grade 8 candidates

- Produce a consistently convincing, informed response to a range of meanings and ideas within the text.
- Use ideas which are well-linked and will often build on one another.
- Dig deep into the text, examining, exploring and evaluating writers' use of language, form and structure.
- Carefully select finely judged textual references which are well integrated in order to support and develop responses to texts.
- Show perceptive understanding of how contexts shape texts and responses to texts.

Achieving a grade 9

To reach the very highest level you need to have thought about the novel more deeply and produce a response which is conceptualised, critical and exploratory at a deeper level. You might, for instance, challenge accepted critical views in evaluating whether the writer has always been successful. If, for example, you think Dickens set out to create sympathy for the poor, how successful do you think he has been?

You may feel that the creation of sympathy for the poor through what might be described as the blatant manipulation of the reader's emotional response to Tiny Tim alienates some modern readers. Does the presentation of Tim verge on sentimentality, and if so do you consider this a problem or not?

You need to make original points clearly and succinctly and convince the examiner that your viewpoint is really your own, and a valid one, with constant and careful reference to the text. This will be aided by the use of short and apposite (really relevant) quotations, skilfully embedded in your answer along the way (see Sample essays on pp. 72–90).

REVIEW YOUR LEARNING

1 On which paper is your *A Christmas Carol* question?

2 Can you take your copy of the novel into the exam?

3 Will you have a choice of questions?

4 How long do you have to answer the question?

5 What advice would you give to another student about using quotations?

6 Will you be assessed on spelling, punctuation and grammar in your response to *A Christmas Carol*?

7 Why is it important to plan your answer?

8 What should you do if you finish ahead of time?

Answers on p. 101.

Assessment Objectives and skills

All GCSE examinations are pinned to specific areas of learning that the examiners want to be sure the candidates have mastered. These are known as Assessment Objectives or AOs. If you are studying *A Christmas Carol* as an examination text for AQA, Eduqas or Edexcel, the examiner marking your exam response will be trying to give you marks, using the particular mark scheme for that board. However, all mark schemes are based on fulfilling the key AOs for English literature.

Assessment Objectives

The Assessment Objectives that apply to your response to *A Christmas Carol* depend on the exam board.

AO1 and AO2: AQA, Eduqas and Edexcel

AO1 **Read, understand and respond to texts.** Students should be able to: • maintain a critical style and develop an informed personal response • use textual references, including quotations, to support and illustrate interpretations **AO2** **Analyse the language, form and structure used by a writer to create meanings and effects, using relevant subject terminology where appropriate.**

AO3: AQA and Eduqas only

AO3 **Show understanding of the relationship between texts and the contexts in which they were written.** If you are entered for the Edexcel examination, AO3 is not assessed on the *A Christmas Carol* question.

AO4

Although AO4 does not apply directly to *A Christmas Carol*, it is still worth mentioning.

AO4 **Use a range of vocabulary and sentence structures for clarity, purpose and effect, with accurate spelling and punctuation.** You cannot forget about AO4 entirely as it will probably be assessed on another part of the paper, usually Section A. That said, if your spelling or punctuation leaves something to be desired, at least you can lift your spirits by reminding yourself that AO4 is only worth about 5% of your total mark.

Skills

Let's break the Assessment Objectives down to see what they really mean.

> **AO1 Read, understand and respond to texts.** Students should be able to:
> - maintain a critical style and develop an informed personal response
> - use textual references, including quotations, to support and illustrate interpretations.

At its most basic level, this AO is about having a good grasp of what a text is about and being able to express an opinion about it within the context of the question. For example, if you were to say: 'The novel is about a mean man called Scrooge' you would be beginning to address AO1 because you have made a personal response. An 'informed' response refers to the basis on which you make that judgement. In other words, you need to show that you know the novel well enough to answer the question.

It is closely linked to the idea that you are also required to '**use textual references including quotations to support and illustrate interpretations'**. This means giving short direct quotations from the text. For example, if you wanted to support the idea that Scrooge could be mean and aggressive, you could use a direct quote to point to the fact that the carol singer 'fled in terror'. Alternatively, you can simply refer to details in the text in order to support your views. So you might say: 'Scrooge is mean and aggressive because he chases away a frozen carol singer.'

Generally speaking, most candidates find AO1 relatively easy. Usually, it is tackled well — if you answer the question you are asked, this Assessment Objective will probably take care of itself.

> **AO2 Analyse the language, form and structure used by a writer to create meanings and effects, using relevant subject terminology where appropriate.**

AO2 is a different matter. Most examiners would probably agree that covering AO2 is a weakness for many candidates, particularly those students who only ever talk about the characters as if they were real people.

In simple terms, AO2 refers to the writer's methods and is often signposted in questions by the word 'how' or the phrase 'how does the writer present...'.

Overall, AO2 is equal in importance to AO1 so it is vital that you are fully aware of this objective. **Language** refers to Dickens's use of words. Remember that writers choose words very carefully in order to achieve particular effects. They may spend quite a long time deciding between two or three words which are similar in meaning in order to create the precise effect that they are looking for.

If you are addressing AO2 in your response to *A Christmas Carol*, you will typically find yourself using Dickens's name and exploring the choices he has made. For example, if you say: 'Dickens describes Scrooge as "tight-fisted"', this will set you on the right path to explaining why his choice of words is interesting. It is this explanation that addresses AO2, while 'Scrooge was tight-fisted' is a simple AO1 comment.

Of course, there is no right or wrong answer, but you might say that not only does tight-fisted have an idiomatic use, suggesting that someone is mean, but it also suggests the idea of a tightly clenched fist which is not only hanging on to every last penny, but also creates the idea of someone who is aggressive and bad tempered. Even the sound of the word is harsh.

Language also encompasses a wide range of writer's methods, such as the use of different types of imagery, words which create sound effects, litotes, irony and so on. AO2 also refers to your use of **'subject terminology'**. This means that you should be able to use terms such as 'metaphor', 'alliteration' and 'hyperbole' with confidence and understanding. However, if you can't remember the term, don't despair — you can still gain marks for explaining the effects being created.

Form refers to the narrative viewpoint of the novel (see p. 48 in the Language, style and analysis section) as well as to more general ideas about the kind or genre of text you are studying. *A Christmas Carol* is quite difficult to classify. You may have seen it referred to as a novella, a work of fiction that is longer than a short story but not as long as a novel such as *Great Expectations* which has 59 chapters. However, longer novellas such as *A Christmas Carol*, are frequently referred to as novels and you will notice that your examination board refers to it as a novel.

It can be seen as an allegory, since the story can be read on two levels: as a rollicking good yarn, but also as a story with a deeper meaning since the characters can be seen as symbols as well as real people. For example, the Ghost of Christmas Past can be interpreted as symbolising memories and Tiny Tim represents poor, innocent Victorian children, victims of an uncaring society.

Another aspect of the novel is the Gothic influence, in that it also deals with the terror of the supernatural. The Victorians were fascinated by ghost stories and particularly associated them with Christmas. In this sense they were part of an older tradition of winter tales to be told around the fire on dark, chilly evenings.

Structure refers to how it has been 'put together' by the writer. This might include the narrative technique being used — in *A Christmas Carol* Dickens uses the third person intrusive narrator; the order of events and the effects created by it; and the way key events are juxtaposed. For example, the description of the dreadful neglected part of the graveyard where Scrooge's lonely tombstone is found follows on from the portrayal of the grieving Cratchit family and Tiny Tim's body lying in a cheerful well-lit room in the family home. It thus offers a powerful contrast. Effects of structure can also be seen in the writer's use of sentence lengths and word order (syntax).

Remember, if you do not address AO2 at all, it will be very difficult to achieve much higher than grade 1, since you will not be answering the question.

AO3   Show understanding of the relationship between texts and the contexts in which they were written.

Although AO3 is perhaps not considered to be as important as AO1 and AO2, is still worth between 15% and 20% of your total mark in the examination as a whole, and so should not be underestimated. However, do remember it is not assessed for this novel if you are entered with Edexcel.

To cover AO3 you must show that you understand the links between a text and when, why and for whom it was written. For example, some awareness of how the poor were treated in Victorian England may well help you to understand Dickens's intentions in writing *A Christmas Carol* to help to change the attitudes of a largely middle-class readership. Equally, some knowledge of Dickens's background might give you useful insight into his concern about the treatment of children in the nineteenth century.

You might also consider literary context. *A Christmas Carol* was written as a winter's tale of which there is a long tradition: a ghostly yarn to be read around the fireside at Christmas time; something to thrill and entertain the family rather than to terrify.

However, it is important to understand that context should not be 'bolted on' to your response for no good reason; you are writing about literature not history.

AO4   Use a range of vocabulary and sentence structures for clarity, purpose and effect, with accurate spelling and punctuation.

AO4 is fairly self-explanatory and it is worth remembering that it is not assessed in your response to *A Christmas Carol*. However, a clear and well-written response should always be your aim. If your spelling is so bad or your grammar and lack of punctuation so confusing that the examiner cannot understand what you are trying to express, this will obviously adversely affect your mark.

Similarly, although there are no marks awarded for good handwriting, and none taken away for untidiness or crossings out, it is obviously important for the examiner to be able to read what you have written. If you believe your handwriting is so illegible that it may cause difficulties for the examiner, you need to speak to your schools examination officer in plenty of time before the exam. He/She may be able to arrange for you to have a scribe or to sit your examination using a computer.

What you will not gain many marks for

- **Retelling the story.** You can be sure that the examiner marking your response knows the story inside out. A key feature of the lowest grades is 'retelling the story'. Don't do it.

- **Quoting long passages.** Remember, the point is that every reference and piece of quotation must serve a very specific point you are making. If you quote at length, the examiner will have to guess which bit of the quotation you mean to serve your point. Don't impose work on the examiner — be explicit about exactly which words you have found specific meaning in. Keep quotes short and smart.

- **Merely identifying literary devices.** You will never gain marks simply for identifying literary devices such as a simile or a use of rhyme. However, you will gain marks by identifying these features, exploring the reasons why you think the author has used them and offering a thoughtful consideration of how they might impact on readers, as well as an evaluation of how effective you think they are.

- **Giving unsubstantiated opinions.** The examiner will be keen to give you marks for your opinions, but only if they are supported by reasoned argument and references to the text.

- **Writing about characters as if they are real people.** It is important to remember that characters are constructs — the writer is responsible for what the characters do and say. Don't ignore the author!

▲ Don't forget the author!

REVIEW YOUR LEARNING

1 What does AO1 assess?
2 What sort of material do you need to cover in order to successfully address AO2?
3 What do you understand by the term AO3?
4 AO4 is not assessed on *A Christmas Carol*, but why is it still important?
5 Which exam board specification are you following and what AOs should you be focusing on?
6 What should you *not* do in your responses?
Answers on p. 101.

The question below is typical of an AQA question, but is similar to an Eduqas question in that it requires you to consider both an extract and the novel as a whole.

First read the question.

This extract from Stave 1 introduces Scrooge to the reader:

Oh! But he was a tight-fisted hand at the grindstone, Scrooge! a squeezing, wrenching, grasping, scraping, clutching, covetous, old sinner! Hard and sharp as flint, from which no steel had ever struck out generous fire; secret, and self-contained, and solitary as an oyster. The cold within him froze his old features, nipped his pointed nose, shrivelled his cheek, stiffened his gait; made his eyes red, his thin lips blue; and spoke out shrewdly in his grating voice. A frosty rime was on his head, and on his eyebrows, and his wiry chin. He carried his own low temperature always about with him; he iced his office in the dog-days; and didn't thaw it one degree at Christmas.

External heat and cold had little influence on Scrooge. No warmth could warm, no wintry weather chill him. No wind that blew was bitterer than he, no falling snow was more intent upon its purpose, no pelting rain less open to entreaty. Foul weather didn't know where to have him. The heaviest rain, and snow, and hail, and sleet, could boast of the advantage over him in only one respect. They often 'came down' handsomely, and Scrooge never did.

Nobody ever stopped him in the street to say, with gladsome looks, 'My dear Scrooge, how are you? When will you come to see me?' No beggars implored him to bestow a trifle, no children asked him what it was o'clock, no man or woman ever once in his life inquired the way to such and such a place, of Scrooge. Even the blind men's dogs appeared to know him; and when they saw him coming on, would tug their owners into doorways and up courts; and then would wag their tails as though they said, 'No eye at all is better than an evil eye, dark master!'

But what did Scrooge care? It was the very thing he liked. To edge his way along the crowded paths of life, warning all human sympathy to keep its distance, was what the knowing ones call 'nuts' to Scrooge.

Starting with this extract, how does Dickens present Scrooge in *A Christmas Carol*?

Write about:

- how Dickens presents Scrooge in this extract
- how Dickens presents Scrooge in the novel as a whole.

You will see below extracts from exam responses from two students working at different levels. They cover much the same points. However, if you look carefully you will be able to see how Student Y takes similar material to that of Student X, but develops it further in order to achieve a higher grade.

In addressing the first bullet, both students looked at the extract and begin by considering how Scrooge's character and appearance are presented in the first paragraph.

Student X, who is likely to achieve grade 5, begins the response like this:

> I am going to explain how Dickens presents Scrooge in the extract and then how Dickens presents Scrooge in the novel as a whole. The writer uses one word sentences and exclamation marks such as 'Oh!' and, 'Scrooge!' to show how strong the writer's feelings are. He then uses a list of six adjectives to describe him. 'A squeezing, wrenching, grasping, scraping, covetous old sinner!' All of these words are to do with being a miser and by using so many, this also creates a strong impression.
>
> He then uses a simile to suggest he is as hard as flint which is a very hard substance, so the reader is beginning to understand that Scrooge has a very hard heart. By comparing him to an oyster, Dickens is suggesting he has a hard shell and no one can get through to him. Even his appearance makes him seem miserly. His pointed nose and shrivelled cheek give him a mean witch-like appearance and his white hair is described as covered in a 'frosty rime'. Dickens is using hyperbole, suggesting the coldness inside him has affected his features and is the reason for his white hair.

1 There are no marks for this kind of introduction. At this point the examiner may well be thinking 'Well get on with it, then'.

2 Some examples of writer's methods given with a hint of effect, e.g. 'to show how strong the writer's feelings are'. Strong feelings of what, however?

3 This 'impression' needs to be explained.

4 Some explanation of effect.

5 Correct use of terminology.

Student Y, who is likely to achieve grade 8, begins like this:

Dickens's description of Scrooge in this extract begins with a short exclamation 'Oh!' suggesting the intensity of the writer's feelings about him almost as if, for a moment, words fail him. A metaphor follows describing Scrooge as 'a tight-fisted hand at the grindstone'. This is clever, as it suggests both aggression and someone who is determined not to let even a small coin slip through his fingers. The sentence which follows supports and develops this idea with the long list of adjectives, used cumulatively to evoke a strong sense of someone who is determined to get as much as he can at almost any cost to others. Words like 'clutching' and 'grasping' suggest an almost claw-like grip, reminiscent of a merciless bird of prey.

The most powerful image in the passage is the simile 'secret, and self contained, and solitary as an oyster'. The repetition of the sibilant 's' sound enhances the sense of secrecy, and the comparison with an oyster is apt. Like an oyster, Scrooge has a hard and ugly exterior. Oysters are difficult to open and the single creature inside has to be prised out. However, oysters can also produce pearls, so perhaps Dickens is hinting that somewhere deep inside of Scrooge there may be a pearl of goodness.

Even his appearance adds further to the impression of his lack of warmth. For example, Dickens tells us that the cold has 'nipped his pointed nose' suggesting both a face and a nature that are unpleasantly sharp. The 'red eyes' and 'blue lips' appear visually cold, but also suggest an unnatural reversion of what one would expect.

1 Immediate explanation of effect created by writer.

2 Beginning to offer alternative interpretations.

3 Beginning to explore language effects.

4 Analyses different possible interpretations of the simile with an appropriately tentative style.

5 Point is original and imaginative.

Both students then go on to consider the way that Dickens uses the weather to present Scrooge.

Student X writes:

> Dickens also uses the weather to present Scrooge as very cold hearted. Dickens states 'No warmth could warm, no wintry weather chill him.' This phrase also suggests that no matter how others behaved towards him he would not alter his own behaviour. This is emphasised by the use of alliteration with the letter 'w' which draws the reader's attention to the statement and suggests the chilliness of the weather.
>
> Dickens again compares him to unpleasant weather when he writes that no wind is 'bitterer' than Scrooge, as the word 'bitterer' can mean both colder and more spiteful. Dickens states that he is, like snow, 'intent upon its purpose' and like rain, he is not open to 'entreaty.' This adds to the idea that he does not care what other people think of him and will not listen to anyone else. The image of cold weather reinforces the idea of a cold, miserable character so the reader can understand why no one likes him.

1 This supports the idea that he has no connection to others but could do with further explanation.

2 Makes use of appropriate subject terminology.

3 Identifies effect of language choice but rather superficially.

4 Some explanation of effect of language choice.

5 By the end of the paragraph has shown clear understanding of the effects of writer's methods on reader.

This is a promising start and would suggest that Student X is working at grade 5 and is demonstrating 'clear understanding'. The response is well focused on the task and there is clear awareness of Dickens's methods and their effects on the reader though these are not always fully explained.

However, an even better response appears below. **Student Y** is working at grade 8. Look carefully and see if you can identify the differences between the two responses.

In this extract, Dickens uses the wintry weather to convey the impossibility of anyone having any influence on Scrooge, symbolised by another hyperbolic statement, 'No warmth could warm, no wintry weather chill him.' Dickens not only suggests Scrooge is unnatural and lacking in humanity, but that he is so obsessed with his own concerns that he is impervious to the feelings of others. This is emphasised by the juxtaposition of the two extremes of temperature within one sentence, as well as the use of alliteration with the letter 'w' which could be seen as having a slightly onomatopoeic effect, recalling the sound of a whistling wind.

The triadic structure in the next sentence further develops this idea by comparing his extreme bitterness to the bitterest wind. The suggestion that 'no falling snow was more intent upon its purpose' implies that Scrooge was so cold, selfish and uninterested in others that only one thing mattered to him: profit. The phrase 'no pelting rain less open to entreaty' confirms his hard heartedness, linking as it does with the later reference to beggars who dare not implore Scrooge to 'bestow a trifle'.

1 Literary terminology is used effectively.

2 Considering alternative interpretations.

3 Clear explanation of method and effect.

4 Effective use of integrated text.

5 Beginning to explore structure within the extract.

This is clearly at a higher level and is beginning to consider Dickens's methods in a thoughtful, developed style.

Both students then go on to write about Scrooge's **lack of interaction with others**.

Student X writes:

1 Student X continues to focus on the task of writing about the presentation of Scrooge.

> Dickens indicates Scrooge's isolation through the examples of ordinary human contact in which he takes no part. Dickens shows that he is avoided by everyone in his community by telling us that 'no beggars implored him to bestow a trifle', 'no children,' asked him the time and 'no man or woman' asked him how he was.
>
> Humour is used in the idea that even the blind men's dogs pull their masters away and the term 'dark master', connects Scrooge to Satan and makes him seem very wicked.
>
> Dickens states it was the 'very thing' Scrooge liked: 'to edge along the crowded paths of life'. The use of the word 'edge' suggests someone who does not wish to mingle, but actually prefers to stay on the outside, and at this point in the story the reader is unlikely to have any sympathy for him. Scrooge here seems to represent the sort of person who has no feelings towards the poorer members of the society.

2 A range of supporting references is used.

3 Beginning to consider the effects of language choices but no detailed analysis of the patterns in the syntax.

4 Beginning to show some understanding of contextual factors.

Again, this answer shows some clear, sustained understanding, but there is room for improvement. It could be improved by giving some further detail on context as seen in the next section of Student Y's response.

Now read the next section of **Student Y's** response:

Dickens develops the idea of Scrooge's social isolation through the examples of ordinary human contact from which he has excluded himself.

Dickens strengthens this negativity by using the word 'nobody' as the first word in the sentence 'Nobody ever stopped him in the street'. The list of examples is a typical Dickensian linguistic feature which, together with the repetition of negatives 'no beggars', 'no children', 'no man or woman' heightens the idea of his total isolation and the sterility of his existence outside of his community.

1 This is an interesting point on syntax, an area which is sometimes overlooked.

Humour is used in the idea that even the blind men's dogs pull their masters away. Although there are satanic overtones to the term 'dark master', this comic exaggeration begins to establish Scrooge as an almost pantomime villain, thus maintaining the light-hearted tone of the passage.

2 Beginnings of insightful analysis of language and effects.

Dickens states it was the 'very thing' Scrooge liked — 'to edge along the crowded paths of life'. This idea is both literal and metaphorical. The use of the word 'edge' suggests he avoids even touching others as he walks through the town, but it also suggests someone who does not wish to mingle on any level through life's journey. It is clear that he actually prefers to stay on the outside of society, and at this point, the reader is unlikely to have any sympathy for him. Dickens here is clearly using Scrooge to represent the more affluent members of Victorian society who turned a blind eye to the problems of the poor.

3 Starting to explore alternative interpretations which would be expected of a candidate aiming at grade 6 or higher.

4 Beginnings of thoughtful consideration of contextual factors.

This response is convincing and there are signs of an exploratory approach. An essay continuing along these lines would certainly be achieving at the highest level.

When addressing the presentation of Scrooge in the novel as a whole, **Student X** has this to say:

In the rest of Stave 1 we see further evidence of Scrooge's mean character and isolation from his community when he bullies Bob and in the way he treats his visitors. Dickens is systematically showing us that Scrooge lacks humanity as an employer, a family member and a member of his community.

1 Clear response to explicit meanings.

Dickens shows how Scrooge begins to change when he is taken to his old schoolroom and regrets chasing the carol singer. His obvious delight at the Fezziwig party suggests that Scrooge regrets his ill treatment of Bob. However, it is in the scenes involving Belle that Dickens shows us a man who now understands exactly what he has lost and cannot bear it.

Dickens shows his developing compassion in his anxiety over whether Tiny Tim will live, and his horror when he is shown the two children Ignorance and Want and has his words thrown back at him — 'Are there no workhouses?'. By the end of Stave 4 he has been given the chance to see his own friendless future and it scares him.

2 Apt textual reference used here.

Finally, in Stave 5, Dickens shows us a completely transformed Scrooge. Dickens presents him as ecstatic with happiness at the prospect of a second chance as he whoops and halloos. Dickens makes it seem like a rebirth as he 'frisked' about saying he was 'quite a baby' and 'as merry as a schoolboy'.

3 Understands how language is used here but could be more fully explained — what exactly is the effect created by 'frisked' for example? New-born lamb, perhaps?

Dickens confirms Scrooge's utter transformation by the fact that he meets all the people he spurned in Stave 1 and acts quite differently towards them, tipping the messenger boy, donating to charity, visiting Fred and giving Bob a raise.

4 Shows a clear understanding of Dickens's use of structure.

Dickens ends the novel with the idea that Scrooge keeps Christmas as well as any man and becomes 'as good a friend, as good a master, as good a man, as the good old city knew'.

5 Clear conclusion reached.

Student X is showing an ability to achieve at grade 5 with this clear, coherent response. The response never strays from the focus of the question and it is obvious that Student X has a solid grasp of the details of the novel as a whole.

Now look at the way **Student Y** approaches the presentation of Scrooge in the novel as a whole:

In the remainder of Stave 1 we see further evidence of Scrooge's miserly character and isolation from his community in his treatment of Bob, the charity collectors, Fred and the carol singer. The systematic depiction of a man who not only lacks humanity as an employer, but also as a family member and a member of his community suggests someone who is beyond redemption, since he seems to care for no one. However, it is part of Dickens's purpose to suggest that no sinner is so miserable that they are beyond redemption.

When Scrooge is taken to his old schoolroom, we see his frozen features begin to thaw as he is apparently moved by his past memories. We see the beginnings of regret for his behaviour, especially his loss of Belle, which perhaps explains his bitterness towards Fred's loving marriage. These scenes are important too because they help the reader to understand that Scrooge was not always the two-dimensional villain of Stave 1. The reader can begin to understand him, a child sent away from home at an early age to an over strict school, abandoned by all except the sister he loved but who died young.

His avaricious nature is partly explained by a fear of the effects of poverty, as he states: 'There is nothing on which [the world] is so hard as poverty.'

Dickens shows Scrooge's developing comprehension of the power employers have over their workers' lives in the visit to the Fezziwigs and, when the Ghost of Christmas Present shows him the Cratchit household, we see compassion in his anxiety over

1 Perceptive understanding of Dickens's intentions.

2 Well-integrated link between the extract and the whole novel.

3 Convincing personal response to an implicit meaning.

4 Judicious reference to a key idea in the novel.

whether Tiny Tim will live, and he is powerfully reminded of his earlier callous comments on the 'surplus population.'

Finally, in Stave 5, Dickens reveals to the reader a completely transformed Scrooge, emphasising this transformation by mirroring the events of Stave 1, by having Scrooge meet those he treated so harshly and making amends, for instance through the donation to the charity workers which contains many 'back-payments.'

5 Perceptive response to Dickens's use of structure.

In total contrast to Stave 1, Dickens now presents Scrooge as ecstatic and almost child-like at the prospect of a second chance, stressing the simple joy Scrooge now feels through a succession of almost clichéd similes, as he 'frisked' about claiming to be 'as merry as a schoolboy' and 'as light as a feather.'

Scrooge becomes 'as good a friend, as good a master, as good a man, as the good old city knew...', the triadic structure in praise of Scrooge and the repetition of the word 'good' emphasising a total transformation from the isolated and unfeeling man in Stave 1.

6 Excellent conclusion linked to perceptive analysis of language.

Throughout the response, Student Y sustains a convincing, thoughtful response which offers a range of interesting interpretations and which covers all the requirements to achieve grade 8, and possibly higher.

The following sample responses are based on an extract question which focuses on a theme, rather than a character. The format for the question is as for Eduqas, but is similar to one that might be set by AQA.

A Christmas Carol

You are advised to spend about 45 minutes on this question.

You should use the extract below and your knowledge of the whole novel to answer this question.

Write about how the importance of family is presented throughout the novel.

In your response you should:

- Refer to the extract and the novel as a whole;
- Show your understanding of characters and events in the novel;
- Refer to the contexts of the novel.

'Here's Martha, mother,' cried the two young Cratchits. 'Hurrah! There's *such* a goose, Martha!'

'Why, bless your heart alive, my dear, how late you are!' said Mrs Cratchit, kissing her a dozen times, and taking off her shawl and bonnet for her with officious zeal.

'We'd a deal of work to finish up last night,' replied the girl, 'and had to clear away this morning, mother!'

'Well never mind so long as you are come,' said Mrs Cratchit. 'Sit ye down before the fire, my dear, and have a warm, Lord bless ye!'

'No, no! There's father coming,' cried the two young Cratchits, who were everywhere at once. 'Hide, Martha, hide!'

So Martha hid herself, and in came little Bob, the father, with at least three feet of comforter exclusive of the fringe, hanging down before him; and his threadbare clothes darned up and brushed, to look seasonable; and Tiny Tim upon his shoulder. Alas for Tiny Tim, he bore a little crutch, and had his limbs supported by an iron frame!

'Why, where's our Martha?' cried Bob Cratchit, looking round.

'Not coming,' said Mrs Cratchit.

'Not coming!' said Bob, with a sudden declension in his high spirits; for he had been Tim's blood horse all the way from church, and had come home rampant. 'Not coming upon Christmas Day!'

Martha didn't like to see him disappointed, if it were only in joke; so she came out prematurely from behind the closet door, and ran into his arms, while the two young Cratchits hustled Tiny Tim, and bore him off into the wash-house, that he might hear the pudding singing in the copper.

Student X, who is hoping to achieve grade 5, begins like this:

1 Gets straight to the point.

4 Simple reference to the writer's method.

> Family is an important theme in 'A Christmas Carol' and in this extract from Stave 3 the reader meets the Cratchit family on Christmas Day when the Ghost of Christmas Present takes Scrooge to see how they celebrate Christmas. The family seem to have a very strong bond as we can see when they greet the oldest sister Martha with Mrs Cratchit 'kissing her a dozen times' and the two young Cratchits shouting 'Hurrah!'. Right from the beginning Dickens is presenting them as a family who care about each other deeply.

2 Shows awareness of the events surrounding the extract, in effect, briefly putting it into context.

3 Appropriate use of textual support, well embedded. Remember to keep quotations, especially from a given extract, short and to the point.

While this is a steady opening paragraph which reveals some clear understanding of the extract, it is not yet demonstrating AO2 skills at the required level. Student X begins to address these skills in the second paragraph:

2 Appropriate supporting detail.

3 Considering the effect on the reader, albeit briefly.

> Dickens presents the importance of family through his description of Bob's arrival with 'Tiny Tim upon his shoulder'. Here the reader feels sympathy for Bob and sees that the father is supporting his crippled son. Also, Bob's concern for his family is then shown by Dickens in the way he is depressed and upset at the idea that his daughter Martha is not coming for Christmas: 'Not coming upon Christmas Day!' Dickens uses an exclamation mark to stress Bob's emotions here.

1 Continued focus on task — it is a good idea to use the 'key word' of the question, in this case 'family', in each paragraph to make it clear that you have focused on the task.

4 Lacking detail perhaps, but clear understanding of Dickens's methods.

The response is certainly improving. Dickens's methods are considered in this paragraph, as are the effects he creates on the reader. Although some points could be developed further, for example the use of exclamation marks, the sense of a grade 5 response is emerging. Student X now offers a final paragraph on the extract itself, before moving on to the novel as a whole.

2 Awareness of Dickens's intentions as a writer.

> The Ghost of Christmas Present is showing Scrooge this picture of a happy family group to make him see the importance of family and also the reality of poverty which he has never experienced. Dickens uses the Cratchits to show how a family supports each other and can celebrate Christmas despite their problems. All the family are shown to get along with each other as Dickens shows us by the way Mrs Cratchit greets her daughter, the way Martha runs into her father's arms, and the way the young Cratchits look after Tiny Tim at the end of the extract.

1 Sense of the purpose of the visit shown here and understanding of context.

3 Clear paraphrasing of details to support a point. There is no need to use quotations all of the time if you can paraphrase like this.

By this stage Student X is close to a grade 5, but now needs to move on to consider the whole novel.

First, however, consider this response to the extract by Student Y who is working at a higher level.

Student Y opens the response as follows:

> In this extract from Stave 3 Dickens presents the reader with a slightly sentimental picture of the idealised Cratchit family on Christmas Day, demonstrating to the reader, and Scrooge, how the dignified poor are still able to celebrate Christmas in a warm, family environment. The family's powerful bond is displayed when the eldest daughter Martha is greeted by Mrs Cratchit 'kissing her a dozen times', Dickens using hyperbole and also the repetition of the word 'bless' to emphasise the love between mother and daughter.

1 Opening sentence shows clear awareness of Dickens's purpose.

2 Well embedded textual support.

3 Appropriate use of technical term.

4 Understanding of both method and effect here.

This is a strong opening paragraph, focused on the task and showing clear understanding of Dickens's methods and intentions. The response continues to focus on the extract:

> The importance of family is further examined by Dickens through his description of Bob's arrival with 'Tiny Tim upon his shoulder'. Here Dickens creates sympathy for 'little' Bob as he is literally supporting his crippled son, an image which may reflect the way Bob is forced to work hard to 'support' his family. Also, Bob's belief in the importance of family is shown by Dickens through his reaction to the idea that his daughter Martha is not coming for Christmas, where the repetition of the phrase 'Not coming...' and the repeated exclamation marks reveal the depth of Bob's feelings of disappointment.

2 Point is developed and linked to the whole novel. Notice the slightly tentative style – 'which may reflect...', often a sign of a considered response.

1 Embedded support and explained effect.

3 Effects of two methods clearly explained — compare this with Student X's comments on the same section of the extract.

By this stage Student Y has covered all the requirements for a grade 5 and is moving into grade 6. One more paragraph is offered on the extract:

1 Considered response to context.

> Although a modern reader might well find this portrayal of the 'perfect' family to be somewhat unrealistic, Dickens's intention is clear: the Ghost of Christmas Present forces Scrooge to witness this happy family group to open his eyes to the importance of family life and also the reality of poverty which Scrooge has never experienced. It is clear that Scrooge is beginning to develop sympathy for the Cratchits as shortly after this extract he asks if Tiny Tim will live and is horrified to have his words about the 'surplus population' thrown back at him by the ghost.

2 Clear understanding of writer's intentions.

3 Excellent knowledge of material beyond the extract, although slightly veering from the point of the question.

Now take a look at the way **Student X** deals with the importance of family in the novel as a whole in the fourth paragraph of his/her response:

2 Shows solid knowledge of characters and events.

> In the novel as a whole, Dickens mainly presents the importance of family through his description of Scrooge and his transformation. In the opening stave we witness Scrooge refusing his nephew Fred's kind offer to join him and his wife for Christmas. As Fred is Scrooge's only living relative, this reveals that Scrooge has no warmth towards his family. He even dismisses the idea that Fred has married because he 'fell in love' and demands to be left alone.

1 Begins to address 'whole novel' with reasonable point.

3 Appropriate, embedded textual support from outside of the extract.

Student X immediately reveals a secure knowledge of events and characters in the novel and links them with the theme of family quite effectively. Despite being a 'closed book' examination, it is good to see some textual support offered.

In the next paragraph Student X considers the 'transformed' Scrooge:

1 Hints at a point on structure here — needs more explanation of exactly how Dickens mirrors events and characters.

> However, in Stave 5 when Scrooge's character has transformed, Dickens contrasts the old Scrooge with the new one by presenting him accepting his family by attending the party at Fred's house. When he arrives he is greeted warmly and made to feel at home, just as a member of the family should. Dickens stresses the enjoyment he feels at being with his family when he writes: 'Wonderful party, wonderful games, won-der-ful happiness!' repeating the word 'wonderful' to emphasise Scrooge's new happiness.

2 Clear knowledge of text — excellent supporting detail.

3 More could be added here on writer's method/effect (see Student Y for how this might be addressed more effectively).

Student X is now operating at a secure grade 5 level, showing a clear understanding of the writer and his ideas and offering an engaged response to the question. The next two paragraphs consider other methods by which Dickens presents the importance of family:

1 Another example of awareness of the whole novel.

> Dickens also uses the Ghost of Christmas Past to bring out the importance of family as the spirit reveals aspects of the miser's earlier life to Scrooge. By showing the reader Scrooge as a lonely schoolboy and hinting that as a boy he had an unhappy family life Dickens might be giving the reader an idea of why Scrooge has ended up with no understanding of the importance of family and this makes us feel some sympathy for him.

2 Moving towards a more considered response?

> However, the Ghost also helps to open Scrooge's eyes to the importance of family by bringing him face to face with his younger sister, Fan, who is described as having a 'large heart' and obviously cared for Scrooge. The reminder that Fan was the mother of Fred makes Scrooge pause to think about how badly he treated his nephew and could be said to begin his understanding of the importance of family.

1 Continuing focus on the task — plenty of references to family.

2 Effective tentative style emerging here — into grade 6 perhaps.

Now read Student X's final paragraph:

> Finally, I would say that the Ghost of Christmas Past is also used by Dickens to show Scrooge what he has lost in terms of family, and this is done through the introduction of Scrooge's ex-fiancée, Belle. The ghost first reminds Scrooge of the reason for Belle breaking off their engagement — he loved money more than her — but then forces Scrooge to see Belle as she is now, as a wife and mother. Belle and her husband and children are presented as an ideal family even though they are not as rich as Scrooge. This brings home the importance of family very clearly to Scrooge and the reader.

1 Fine to use the first person here.

2 Shows a clear understanding of Dickens's message.

3 Effective ending, retaining clear focus on family.

Overall, Student X clearly fulfils the requirements for grade 5, even edging towards grade 6 in places. You might notice that the response is approximately 700 words in length. A good response does not have to be long; just make sure it is focused on the question.

Now consider how **Student Y** dealt with the 'whole novel' element of the question:

1 Cleverly linking the extract to the novel as a whole.

This cosy picture of family life which Dickens portrays through the Cratchits is clearly designed to serve as a powerful contrast to Scrooge's lack of interest in anything pertaining to family. The Cratchits' family Christmas may well remind the reader of what Scrooge is missing through his refusal to accept his nephew Fred's invitation to spend Christmas Day with him and his wife. Given that Fred is Scrooge's only living relative, his disdain towards him reveals that Scrooge has no warmth towards his family. Dickens presents Scrooge as contemptuous of the notion that Fred has married because he 'fell in love', perhaps suggesting that Scrooge is jealous of Fred's marriage, particularly given what we learn of Belle and Scrooge's relationship later in the novel.

2 Well explained effect on the reader.

3 Interesting alternative interpretation.

Dickens uses the cyclical structure of the novel to provide contrast in Stave 5 when the reader sees Scrooge's character transformed. The new, almost reborn, Scrooge thinks first of the Cratchit family, seeking to improve their day with his gift of a 'prize turkey', and then is presented by Dickens as accepting of his own family by attending the party at Fred's house, where he is greeted warmly and without recriminations by Fred, who almost shakes his arm off, and is made to feel 'at home in five minutes'. The importance of family and the ecstatic enjoyment Scrooge feels is emphasised by Dickens in the words 'Wonderful party, wonderful games, won-der-ful happiness!' Scrooge's repeating of the word 'wonderful' suggesting not only his joy but also perhaps the idea that he is almost lost for words.

1 Good awareness of the structure of the novel.

2 Unusual point on family — evidence of independent thought, perhaps?

3 Excellent knowledge of text for support.

4 Offers alternative interpretations of effects created by Dickens's language.

1 Well linked to previous paragraph.

However, it is not just in the description of Scrooge's transformation that Dickens shows us the importance of family; Dickens also uses the Ghost of Christmas Past to bring out the importance of family by presenting Scrooge, and the reader, with evidence from Scrooge's formative years. We are made aware of Scrooge as a lonely schoolboy whose only solace comes from his reading, and we are given hints by his younger sister, Fan, that his family life is far from ideal, especially when his father is described as 'kinder than he used to be' and it is suggested that as a boy Scrooge rarely went home for Christmas. This picture of an unhappy family life seems designed to give the reader some insight into Scrooge's unfeeling nature as an adult and creates some sympathy for him.

2 Excellent detailed knowledge of events of the novel.

3 Clear analysis of method and effect.

By bringing the present-day Scrooge face to face with his late sister in this way, Dickens is able to show the beginnings of a change in Scrooge and a suggestion that he is beginning to understand the importance of family. Fan is presented as a loving girl with a 'large heart' and a strong belief in family, and Scrooge is pressed by the ghost to acknowledge that she was the mother of his nephew. This realisation makes him 'uneasy in his mind', a hint of his growing guilt at the harsh treatment of Fred in Stave 1 perhaps.

4 A well-developed and thoughtful response to the purpose of Fan in the novel.

Now read **Student Y's** final paragraph:

The Ghost of Christmas Past reminds Scrooge of his earlier life but is also used by Dickens in Stave 2 to reveal what Scrooge has lost in terms of family through his obsessions with money and business. This is achieved through the introduction of Scrooge's ex-fiancée, Belle. Having first revealed to us how Scrooge came to lose Belle through his 'pursuit of wealth', the ghost then forces Scrooge to witness the now married Belle with her children. Belle, her loving husband and their lively children are presented, like the Cratchits in the extract, as an ideal family. Even though they are not as wealthy as Scrooge and their home is not large, it is 'full of comfort'. This brings home the importance of family very powerfully to Scrooge and he cannot bear to see any more, clearly suggesting that he is now realising the importance of family over money.

1 Flowing effectively into the next paragraph.

2 Links back to the extract and shows awareness of patterns in the novel.

3 Strong conclusion, well focused on task.

Student Y has produced a considered and thoughtful response with impressive, detailed support and some interesting alternative interpretations. Grade 8 is certainly achieved here.

Top ten

As your examination will be 'closed book' and you will only have a short extract in front of you, you might find it helpful to memorise some quotations to use in support of your points in the examination response, particularly when addressing the question in the rest of the novel. See the Tackling the exams section on pp. 57–66 for further information about the format of the examination.

You don't need to remember long quotations; short quotes that you can embed into a sentence will be more effective. If all else fails, as long as you can remember the gist of what the quotation relates to, you can use a textual reference.

Top ten characterisation quotations

The following quotations can be used as a quick reminder of the way that Dickens has presented the key characteristic of each of the main characters.

Scrooge

...secret, and self contained, and solitary as an oyster. (p. 8)

- A powerful simile using sibilance to describe his wilful isolation as an adult.

1

'...every idiot who goes about with "Merry Christmas" on his lips should be boiled with his own pudding, and buried with a stake of holly through his heart.' (p. 10)

- A humorous indication of his hatred of Christmas.

2

Darkness is cheap, and Scrooge liked it. (p. 17)

- The indicates his miserliness and links him with darkness and evil.

3

> **GRADE BOOSTER**
>
> If you find that you can't remember a full quotation, try and remember its main message. For example, in the first quotation below, you could just state that Scrooge is compared to an oyster. You could then still use this idea to explain that perhaps Dickens is suggesting that Scrooge has a hard exterior and is difficult to get through to, while also implying that there might be a pearl of goodness within him.

Bob

4 ...the clerk's fire was so very much smaller that it looked like one coal. (p. 9)
- A simile to suggest Bob's working conditions, which were not untypical of the time.

5 ...ran home to Camden Town as hard as he could pelt, to play at blindman's-buff. (p. 15)
- This suggests a playful family man.

6 '...Mr Scrooge, the Founder of the feast!' (p. 56)
- This indicates his generous nature.

Marley's ghost

7 'I wear the chain I forged in life...' (p. 22)
- A powerful symbol of how man can be weighed down by greed and lack of compassion.

8 'Why did I walk through crowds of fellow-beings with my eyes turned down...' (p. 23)
- Dickens uses Marley's Ghost to enhance his message about the importance of community.

Fred

'...the only time I know of...when men and women seem by one consent to open their shut-up hearts freely, and to think of people below them as if they really were fellow-passengers to the grave,...' (p. 11)

9

- Fred's love of Christmas is used to contrast with Scrooge's hatred of it.

Let him in? It is a mercy he didn't shake his arm off. (p. 88)

10

- This reveals the strength of Fred's open-handed and hearty welcome to Scrooge.

GRADE *BOOSTER*

Another useful method is to record quotations onto your iPod and play them over and over. Or you might try watching one of the many adaptations to spot where a quote appears. This can be an effective method as you have both sound and vision to help you, and you can see the quotation in context.

Top ten thematic quotations

Isolation

'Scrooge took his melancholy dinner in his usual melancholy tavern;...' (p. 15)

1

- Repetition of the word melancholy emphasises Scrooge's sad and lonely existence.

Nobody ever stopped him in the street to say with gladsome looks, 'My dear Scrooge, how are you?' (p. 8)

2

- Scrooge has apparently driven away all those who would offer ordinary human contact.

He lay, in the dark empty house, with not a man, a woman or a child, to say that he was kind to me in this or that... (p. 76)

3

- When Scrooge 'dies', no one regrets his passing; many Victorians would have been horrified by this idea, given the importance placed on mourning at that time.

The importance of family

4 '...and when he thought that such another creature...might have called him father...' (pp. 42–43)

- Scrooge reflects with sadness on what he has lost through valuing money above marriage and family.

5 '...and Peter might have known...the inside of a pawnbroker's. But they were happy, grateful, pleased with one another...' (p. 57)

- This highlights the idea that the Cratchits, although poor, are very happy.

Poverty

6 'If they would rather die,' said Scrooge,' they had better do it, and decrease the surplus population.' (p. 13)

- This reflects the callous attitude of many wealthy Victorians.

7 The ways were foul and narrow; the shops and houses wretched; the people half-naked, drunken, slipshod, ugly. (p. 71)

- This shows readers the social reality of deprivation.

8 From the folding of its robe, it brought two children; wretched, abject, frightful, hideous, miserable. (p. 66)

- This drives home Dickens's message as Scrooge is confronted by the ugliness of Want and Ignorance.

The meaning of Christmas

9 'What's Christmas time to you but a time for paying bills without money...' (p. 10)

- Scrooge attempts to justify his intense dislike of the festive season.

10 '...though it has never put a scrap of gold or silver in my pocket, I believe it has done me good, and will do me good; and I say, God bless it!' (p. 11)

- Dickens contrasts the much less mercenary views of Fred with Scrooge's hatred of the season.

Ten top quotes in Scrooge's transformation

These quotations will help you to see at a glance the path that Scrooge takes towards his redemption.

It was the very thing he liked. To edge his way along the crowded paths of life, warning all human sympathy to keep its distance... (p. 9)

1

- This reveals Scrooge's determination to avoid human contact.

'There's more of gravy than the grave about you...' (p. 20)

2

- A sceptical Scrooge attempts to dispel the tension created by Marley's visit with humour.

'Your lip is trembling,' said the ghost. 'And what is that upon your cheek?' (p. 30)

3

- The reader discerns the first sign of emotion in Scrooge, evoked by the memories of his past.

'I should like to be able to say a word or two to my clerk just now.' (p. 39)

4

- Scrooge is beginning to understand his effect on the lives of others.

'Spirit!' said Scrooge in a broken voice, 'remove me from this place.' (p. 43)

5

- Both Scrooge and the reader have seen what Scrooge has lost after seeing Belle and her family.

'Spirit,' said Scrooge, with an interest he had never felt before, 'tell me if Tiny Tim will live.' (p. 55)

6

- Scrooge understands the reality of living with poverty and feels genuine compassion.

'This boy is ignorance. This girl is Want. Beware them both, and all of their degree, but most of all beware this boy, for on his brow I see that written which is Doom...' (p. 67)

7

- Scrooge encounters the shocking reality of Ignorance and Want beneath the festive facade.

'No, Spirit! Oh, no, no!' (p. 82)

8

- Repetition of 'no' plus double exclamation marks expresses Scrooge's horror at seeing his own lonely, neglected grave.

9 'The Spirits of all Three shall strive within me. I will not shut out the lessons that they teach.' (p. 83)

- This shows Scrooge's determination to redeem himself.

10 '...it was always said of him, that he knew how to keep Christmas well, if any man alive possessed the knowledge.' (p. 89)

- This reflects the complete and utter change in Scrooge from the miser who hated Christmas at the beginning of the novel.

Wider reading

Fiction

- Dickens, C. (1997) *Complete Ghost Stories*, Wordsworth Classics.
- Dickens, C. (1995) *Christmas Books,* Wordsworth Classics.
- Dickens, C. (1992) 'The story of the Goblins who stole a sexton' in *The Pickwick Papers* (a precursor to *A Christmas Carol*), Wordsworth Classics.

Non-fiction

- Callow, S. (2012) *Charles Dickens*, HarperPress.
- Standiford, L. (2011) *The Man Who Invented Christmas: How Charles Dickens's 'A Christmas Carol' Rescued His Career and Revived Our Holiday Spirits,* Broadway Books.
- Tomalin, C. (2012) *Charles Dickens: A Life* (particularly Chapter 10), Penguin.

Useful websites

- **www.charlesdickenspage.com/carol.html**

  David Perdue's page on *A Christmas Carol*. This is part of a larger website dedicated to Dickens. In this part of the site you can find a plot synopsis, Dickens's printing expenses and profits for the first year of *A Christmas Carol,* illustrations by John Leech and a range of interesting information on subjects such as Sabbatarianism and the plight of the poor as well as the preface to the original edition in Dickens's own hand.

- **www.victorianweb.org/authors/dickens/xmas/pva13.html**

  'Charles Dickens's *A Christmas Carol*, 1843: an introduction': an interesting contextual insight into what prompted Dickens to write the novel as well as material on the structure and themes of *A Christmas Carol*.

- **www.bbc.co.uk/victorianchristmas/history.shtml**

  An essay about the origins of Christmas in Victorian Britain.

- **www.c19.sunygeneseoenglish.org**

  A useful essay that explores adaptations of works by Dickens including *A Christmas Carol,* as well as some interesting and easy-to-read biographical material.

- **www.victorianweb.org/authors/dickens/xmas/pva63.html**

  'The man who invented Christmas': an exploration of how our modern ideas of Christmas have been influenced by those portrayed by Dickens in the novel.

- **http://academic.brooklyn.cuny.edu/english/melani/novel_19c/thackeray/angel.html**

  This site explains the term 'the Angel in the House' which was originally coined by the poet Coventry Patmore in a poem which holds up the Victorian ideal of the virtuous wife. This is particularly relevant to Dickens's 'angels' such as Belle and Caroline (see p. 30).

Answers to *Review your learning* questions

Context (p. 8)

1 Context refers to the social, historical and literary factors that, in the case of *A Christmas Carol*, influenced Dickens's thinking as he wrote, including any events in his own life.
2 Having to go to work in the blacking factory.
3 The novel combines realism in descriptions of poverty but also has some fairy tale elements such as the three spirits.
4 You could be sent to the workhouse.
5 The Industrial Revolution meant that people went to the city to find work in factories.
6 Education.
7 By positive portrayals of happy, family Christmases — Belle, Fred and the Cratchits in particular.
8 The Ghost of Christmas Present.
9 A ghost story set in a town rather than in castles and forests.
10 Robert Malthus.

Plot and structure (p. 16)

1 Marley is dead, Scrooge is mean. Marley warns Scrooge to change his ways and warns him of the arrival of three spirits.
2 The carol singer, Fred and the charity collectors.
3 He shows us what fate awaits Scrooge and prepares us for further supernatural events.
4 To help us to understand why he is the way he is.
5 Because he wishes he had a daughter like her and knows he could have done if he had stayed with Belle.
6 The Cratchits.
7 Ignorance and Want.
8 His own.
9 Scrooge's death comes shortly after the description of Tiny Tim's final resting place, which is very different from Scrooge's, a pleasant green place rather than an overcrowded neglected churchyard.
10 Scrooge meets with the same people in reverse order and the story begins and ends in his chambers.

Characterisation (p. 26)

1 For applauding Fred's positive view of Christmas.
2 A list of powerful adjectives.
3 It is cheap!
4 The dignified poor.
5 '...dismal, little cell'.
6 It symbolises the obsession he had with business when he was alive.
7 Fred.
8 The Ghost of Christmas Past 'shines a light' on Scrooge's past, gives the reader insight into Scrooge's earlier life and represents the importance and nature of memories.
9 Through the descriptions of Ignorance and Want, who hide beneath his robes.
10 The Ghost of Christmas Yet to Come is faceless, silent and inspires fear.

Themes (p. 36)

1 A theme is an idea which the writer explores through plot, structure, characterisation and description. Often a theme is to encourage the reader to change his/her thinking.
2 A theme is a big central idea explored by the writer while a motif is a recurring idea or object.
3 Poverty, isolation, family and Christmas.
4 To raise awareness and to persuade readers to be kinder to the poor.
5 '...secret, and self-contained, and solitary as an oyster'.
6 Family life is always seen positively.
7 Family celebrations, food and drink, music and giving to charity.
8 Time, light and dark, heat and cold.
9 Both are dark and poorly heated.
10 The darkness of his soul and his ignorance.

Language, style and analysis (p. 48)

1 Third-person intrusive.
2 Metaphor and simile.
3 Personification is a form of metaphor where an abstract idea or an inanimate object is given human characteristics.
4 Litotes is deliberate understatement, usually for humorous effect.
5 Hyperbole is deliberate overstatement or exaggeration.
6 To create a sense of drama or to symbolise Scrooge's ignorance.

7 With Tiny Tim's body in a brightly lit room.

8 The London streets, Scrooge's chambers, old Joe's shop (you might also mention the Fezziwig party or the graveyard where Scrooge is buried).

9 Irony.

10 Simple sentences reflect the frugal lifestyle of Scrooge.

Tackling the exams (p. 57)

1 For AQA, Paper 1, and for Edexcel and Eduqas Paper 2.

2 No.

3 No.

4 For AQA and Eduqas, approximately 45 minutes. For Edexcel, 55 minutes.

5 Quotations are a good way of supporting a point. They do not need to be long, and ideally should be embedded in your work.

6 No.

7 It will help you to organise your thoughts and avoid a muddle.

8 Check your work to make sure you have done your very best.

Assessment Objectives and skills (p. 67)

1 Your understanding of the text and your ability to support your ideas.

2 You need to write about how the writer uses language, form and structure to create effects.

3 AO3 refers to the relationship between texts and the contexts in which they were written.

4 AO4, which refers to spelling, punctuation and grammar, is still important because your meaning needs to be clear.

5 Own answers for exam board. Assessment objectives: for AQA and Eduqas AO1, AO2 and AO3; for Edexcel part (a) AO2, part (b) AO1.

6 You should not retell the story, quote at length, simply identify devices without explaining their effects, offer unsupported opinions, or write about characters as if they were real. Remember to avoid these and you won't go far wrong!